Well Done, Good and Faithful Servant

How to hear those words when you meet Jesus face to face

Well Done, Good and Faithful Servant

WELL DONE, GOOD AND FAITHFUL SERVANT

HOW TO HEAR THOSE WORDS WHEN YOU MEET JESUS FACE TO FACE

CHARLES KENNETH

Well Done, Good and Faithful Servant by Charles Kenneth
Copyright © 2021 by Charles Kenneth
All Rights Reserved.
ISBN: 978-1-59755-664-4

Published by: ADVANTAGE BOOKS™ www.advbookstore.com

This book and parts thereof may not be reproduced in any form, stored in a retrieval system or transmitted in any form by any means (electronic, mechanical, photocopy, recording or otherwise) without prior written permission of the author, except as provided by United States of America copyright law.

Unless otherwise indicated, Scripture quotations are taken from the Holy Bible, New King James Version. Copyright 1982 by Thomas Nelson. Used by permission. All rights Reserved.

Scripture marked (NIV) are taken from the Holy Bible, New International Version. Copyright 1973, 1978, 1984 by International Bible Society. Used by permission of Zondervan. All Rights Reserved.

Scripture marked (NLT) are taken from the Holy Bible, New Living Translation. Copyright 1996, 2004, 2015 by Tyndale House Foundation. Used by permission of Tyndale House Publishers. All Rights Reserved.

Scripture marked (NASB) are taken from the Holy Bible, New American Standard Version. Copyright 1960 1962, 1963, 1968, 1971, 1972, 1973, 1975, 1977, 1995 by The Lockman Foundation. All Rights Reserved.

Scripture marked (KJV) are taken from the Holy Bible, King James Version. Public domain.

Scripture marked (AMP) are taken from the Amplified Bible. Copyright 1954, 1958, 1962, 1964, 1965, 1987 by the Lockman Foundation. Used by permission.

Library of Congress Catalog Number: 2021950642

Names:	Kenneth, Charles, Author
Title:	Well Done, Good and Faithful Servant: How to hear those words when you meet Jesus face to face. / Charles Kenneth
Description	Advantage Books, 2021
Identifiers:	ISBN (print): 9781597556644, (mobi, epub): 9781597556781
Subjects:	Christian Life: Inspirational

First Printing January 2022
22 23 24 25 26 27   10 9 8 7 6 5 4 3 2 1

Table of Contents

FOREWORD 7

INTRODUCTION 11

1: ONE MUST BE A TRUE BELIEVER 21

2: ONE MUST TURN FROM THEIR SIN 29

3: KNOW THE MASTER AND HIS BUSINESS 39

4: LIVE YOUR LIFE AS A SACRIFICE TO GOD 49

5: MAKE PRAYER A PRIORITY IN YOUR LIFE 59

6: LOVE ONE ANOTHER 71

7: DO GOOD WORKS 81

8: GIVE 91

9: BE A GOOD MANAGER OF WHAT YOU HAVE RECEIVED 101

10: COME OUT OF THE WORLD AND BE SEPARATE 113

11 PATIENTLY ENDURE SUFFERING 123

12: ONE MUST REMAIN FAITHFUL TO THE END 133

APPENDIX 153

FOOTNOTES / ASTERISKS 161

Well Done, Good and Faithful Servant

Foreword

Truth be told, there were two versions of the forward for this book. I wrote one before I started, and this one after the book had been completed. So, to call it a forward is really a misnomer. It is an afterword that is being placed at the beginning. I did that because once the book was finished, the necessity to write the forward over again became evident, and the reason is a profound one. In writing this book, God showed me how incredibly important it is for every person in His church to want to hear the words, "Well done, good and faithful servant," when they meet Jesus for the first time if the church is going to function as it should in this world.

That may sound strange to some. Why wouldn't a believer want to hear those words from Jesus when they meet Him for the first time? However, I know there are many in the church that either don't think about it, don't care, or don't understand how much is required to hear those words. How do I know? Well, the main reason I know is because the church has become so weak in the last fifty years because every believer has not been living their lives in a way to try to hear those words from Jesus when they meet Him for the first time. There is another reason though, and it seems like this kind of thinking is becoming more and more prevalent in the church.

There are many people who say they don't need or want anything from God when they get to heaven, they'll just be happy to be there. On the surface that sounds very humble, and I agree with the second part of that statement. I will be extremely happy to go to heaven instead of hell, as those are the only two choices a person has. But there is a problem with that kind of thinking, and it is this. That kind of attitude is not going to get a believer very far in fulfilling God's will for them, either in this life or for eternity; and most believers that think that way don't understand what God's will is for them.

God's will for every person in the church who comes to receive His saving grace through faith in His Son Jesus is to grow up in their faith over the course of their lives, and eventually become like His Son, in this life…now. The very word for 'church' in the original Greek language in which the New Testament was written (and where we find all references of the word 'church' in the Bible) is ekklesia, and it means a group of people that are called out for a separate purpose. Called out from where and for what purpose? Called out from the world with the purpose of acting as representatives from heaven, and from God, on this earth. We do this because that's what Jesus did, and the best way to do it is to imitate Jesus.

Now we know, and God knows too, that we are not going to be able to do that perfectly or anything even close to perfectly in this life, but that doesn't mean it still isn't God's will for us, because it is. In fact, you will see in examples given from God's Word in this book that He wants every believer to become equal in strength of faith and in their commitment to Him, so that His church will be the very best witness it can be in this world regarding God's saving grace that is available to anyone through faith in Christ.

The only way every believer is going to become equal in the strength of their faith and their commitment to God is if every believer has the same goal; and that goal should be to hear, "Well done, good and faithful servant," when they meet Jesus for the first time. However, in order to hear those words, it's going to require a level of faith and commitment to God that just isn't there if the goal is only to get to heaven. It is for this reason, and the overall decline of the church, that this book was written. To try to help as many people as possible in the church get back to doing the things they need to do if they want to hear those words when they meet Jesus for the first time.

Before I began working on this project, I went looking online for a book (or many books) that may have already been written on the subject. And I must say, I was surprised when I couldn't find one. At first, I couldn't believe it. That no one would have thought to write a book on such an important subject. However, after beginning to write the book, it occurred to me that the reason no one has probably written anything of its kind is not because no one thought about it, but rather no one wanted to put themselves in the position of potentially being a hypocrite by not practicing everything they are telling others they should be doing.

Foreword

That is a real danger. Jesus absolutely excoriated the Pharisees in places like Matthew chapter 23 and Luke chapter 11 for not practicing what they preach. So to write a book of this kind does, in a way, put an added responsibility on myself to do the things written in it. However, since everything that will be presented comes from God's Word, and we all have a responsibility to follow His Word, I don't feel the added responsibility to myself will be much more than that of yours. Because once you know the things contained in this book, the responsibility for you to do them will be the same as mine if we both want to hear, "Well done, good and faithful servant," when we meet Jesus for the first time.

So where do those words come from in the Bible? These words of praise come from a parable in Matthew chapter 25 where Jesus describes what the kingdom of heaven is like in regards to what a person will both have, and do there. And the parable teaches a lot of very important lessons that all believers should understand. Jesus tells of a Master (spoiler alert, the master is Him) who is going away for a while so He calls His servants and gives them part of what is His and expects them to grow what they are given so that when the Master returns, they can show that they have been faithful to Him.

When the Master does return, He calls each servant and asks them to give an account of what they did with what they were given. The first servant says he doubled what he was given, and the second servant doubled what she was given. The Master's reply to both of them was, *"Well done, good and faithful servant; you were faithful over a few things, I will make you ruler over many things. Enter into the joy of your Lord."* (verses 21, 23)

The third servant, however, did not grow what he was given. In fact, he didn't even try to do anything with what he was given. He just buried it in the ground until the Master returned. The Master was very upset with that servant, took what he had been given, gave it to the one that grew what he was given the most, and threw that third 'wicked' servant out of His presence into the darkness.

Now, this parable has many implications for believers in Jesus Christ, and we will go over the parable a bit more in chapter nine, as well as what those implications are. But for now, let us focus on a couple things. First, obviously a believer in Christ wants to be like one of the first two servants when they finally meet the Master Jesus face to face, and not like the third who gets thrown out of the Masters' presence into the darkness where there will be 'weeping and gnashing of teeth' (verse 30).

Second, and do not miss this. To be a servant of the Master, and to be given gifts before the Master goes away, implies those servants were *already* associated with the Master; they were believers. They were in His service and knew Him as Lord. In the parable, the third servant said he 'knew Him' (verse 24). This has huge implications for believers in Christ who think they can disobey their Lord and Savior up until the time when He either comes back or they go to see Him through death and think everything will be ok between Him and them; because it won't. Suffice to say, there are many things believers need to be doing while their Master Jesus is away, especially if they want to hear "Well done, good and faithful servant" when they see Him for the first time.

There is a sense of urgency though, as it appears we do not have much time left. In the original forward for this book, I wrote more about this and referenced another book that has this author's name on it called How Much Time Has God Given This World. It was my intention to use some of the material from that book in this one, but what has been done instead is if anything is said where the question or comment is answered or expounded upon in greater detail in the other book, then an asterisk (*) is noted and a reference added on where to find that information.

Ok, time to read more about the decline of the church, what it will take to get the church back on track, and more importantly, what every believer will need to do if they want to hear those words of praise from Jesus when they meet Him for the first time.

Introduction

The first time we see the word church in the Bible is in Matthew, chapter 16, where Jesus tells His disciple Peter that he is the one upon whom He will begin to build His church (eklessia). This prophecy was later fulfilled when Peter gave a speech to a large crowd of people in Jerusalem, proclaiming what Jesus did to save them from their sins (the gospel). He urged them to repent and be saved and the Bible says about 3,000 people believed that day, thus beginning the church of God (Acts 2:14-41).

The book of Acts then goes on to give testimony to the powerful effect the church had on the rest of the world. Describing how it grew, what some in the church like the apostle Paul did in their efforts to spread the good news of the gospel, and how the church began to change the world. The church was so powerful that despite Rome's repeated attempts to crush them, Christianity eventually became the only religion allowed in Rome. Emperor Theodosius made the decree in 380AD that the official (and only) religion allowed in Rome was Christianity.

Sadly, it was from that point where the church really began to lose its power and lose its way. Up until that time, the teachings of the church were pure, based on the absolute truth of God's Word the Bible, and those who adhered to that truth were persecuted which served to increase their faith. Yes, we see in the letters from the apostles in the Bible that believers needed to be on their guard against false teachings hundreds of years earlier as well. However, once the persecution of the church stopped and people were actually forced to convert to Christianity, the potential for false teachings to really take hold and corrupt the Word of God increased exponentially.

God has never forced the gift of His saving grace through faith on anyone, then or now. So, it would make sense that when Rome began to force people to 'convert' to Christianity, it was very often a false conversion, not genuine, and with those false conversions the people would bring into the church their ideas, traditions and teachings that are not found in the Bible. Also, without the threat of being persecuted for their beliefs anymore, believers began to assimilate themselves into a world from which they are called to come out and be separate (2 Corinthians 6:17).

This decline of the church continued for hundreds of years, with so called Christians killing other people because they didn't believe in 'their God' who was really no God at all, but one that was made up to suit their own wickedness. This continued until the First and Second Great Awakenings of the eighteenth and nineteenth centuries where God called His church back to being more like the church of Peter and Paul's time; and for a while the church regained much of its power and changed the world again. This led to the birth of America, and many good and wonderful things happened because the church had once again found its way.

The church of Peter and Paul's time, or 'the early church' as it has been called, was the church described in Acts and later in Paul's letters; and has always been the model God intends to use for His church. The 12 steps described in this book are taken from that model, and those who follow them will assure themselves of hearing, "Well done, good and faithful servant," when they meet Jesus for the first time.

However, the church that came out of the First and Second Great Awakenings has lost its power and lost its way again for the same reason it did before. From about the time of the Great Depression the church began to slowly assimilate itself into the world again, and is now in a state of weakness in the effect it has on America and on the world.

So what happened to the church that caused it to assimilate itself into the world, resulting in its current state of weakness and loss of power? The weak state of the church is largely the result of several things that it forgets when it becomes too much like the world. The people of the church have forgotten who God is, we have forgotten who we are in relation to God, we have forgotten who we are in relation to each other, and we have forgotten what our purpose is on the earth. The people of the church have forgotten these things because they do not devote enough time to studying God's Word, nor do they fear God. There's no way to sugar coat it, and it shouldn't be sugarcoated anyway.

The people of the church have forgotten who God is -

Introduction

- We have forgotten that God spoke everything in the universe into existence (Psalm 33:6), how awesome the power of God is to be able to make everything appear from nothing (Hebrews 11:3), by using only words from His mouth (Psalm 33:7, Hebrews 11:3)
- We have forgotten God created so many stars that even with incredibly powerful telescopes we still don't know how many there are. But God knows, and He has a name for each star (Psalm 147:4)
- We have forgotten God set the boundaries of the oceans, that they are not allowed to pass (Job 38:11), and that God has walked on the bottom of the oceans (Job 38:16)
- We have forgotten that God made everything through His wisdom and understanding (Jeremiah 10:12)
- We have forgotten God can stop the rotation of the earth (Joshua 10:12-13), and did so one time because a single person prayed to Him (verse 14)
- We have forgotten our very breath comes from God, it's His, and if He were to take it back all flesh on earth would die (Job 34:14-15)
- We have forgotten God knows how many hairs are on our heads (Matthew 10:30)
- We have forgotten nothing is hidden from God's sight, and that everyone will give an account one day of how they lived their life (Hebrews 4:13)
- We have forgotten nothing is too hard for the Lord God (Genesis 18:14)

How can it be that most Christians go about their daily lives giving little or no thought about a God like this? (1) How can it be that less than 25% of Christians attend Sunday services regularly where they can learn more about a God like this? (2)

The people of the church have also forgotten who we are in relation to God –

- We have forgotten we were chosen by God before He created the world (Ephesians 1:4), through the foreknowledge of God (1 Peter 1:2), predestined to believe in Jesus (Acts 13:48), chosen for salvation through sanctification by the Holy Spirit (2 Thessalonians 2:13)

- We have forgotten God lives inside us (John 14:17), inside our hearts (2 Corinthians 1:22), through the indwelling of the Holy Spirit (Romans 8:11)

- We have forgotten this indwelling makes each one of us a temple for the Almighty God (1 Corinthians 3:16), and because we are a temple for the Holy Spirit, we are not our own anymore (1 Corinthians 16:19); because Jesus bought us at huge cost through His death on the cross (v 20)

- We have forgotten that because we are now His, we are part of Jesus, part of His flesh and His bones (Ephesians 5:30)

- We have forgotten because we are one with Jesus through faith in Him, we have also been given His righteousness (2 Corinthians 5:21). Righteousness means right standing with God (Romans 5:21, 8:30, NLT)

- We have forgotten that our right standing with God gives us special access to Him (Romans 5:2)

- We have forgotten that without this right standing only one person, the High Priest of Israel, could come before God once a year (Hebrews 9:7), but we have access through the blood of Jesus at any time (Hebrews 10:19)

- We have forgotten that because of our righteous position with God, He will not destroy a city if only ten of us are in it (Genesis 18:32), even if only one person righteous through faith is in it (Ezekiel 22:30)

Introduction

Think about that for a moment. If you are a true believer in Christ, God will not destroy the city you live in simply because you are there! In fact, God will not destroy the world right now because you are there. Noah was the only righteous person in the world before God destroyed it with a flood (Hebrews 11:7), yet He saved Noah in the ark, and He will not destroy the world with you in it either; because the Lord God does not change (Malachi 3:6).

How can it be that less than 20% of Christians say their faith in God, who *will not destroy the world* simply because they are in it, is their highest priority in life?! (3) How can it be that only 2% of Christians say it is their main goal to have a better relationship with a God like this?! (4)

The people of the church have also forgotten who we are in relation to each other –

- We have forgotten that we are all part of each other, one body in Christ (1 Corinthians 12:12-13)

- We have forgotten that we all have an important part to play within our one body (1 Corinthians 12:18)

- We have forgotten we have all been given spiritual gifts to build up the body of Christ (Ephesians 4:16)

- We have forgotten that when one believer suffers, our whole body suffers (1 Corinthians 12:26, Hebrews 13:3)

- We have forgotten that we are to put the needs of others within our body in Christ first (Romans 12:10, Philippians 2:3)

- We have forgotten that we are to love one another in the body of Christ as Jesus loved us (John 13:34)

- We have forgotten that as Jesus came to serve and not to be served (Matthew 20:28), and so those in the church should also serve one another (Galatians 5:13)

- We have forgotten that we should share everything we have with one another in our body in Christ so that there will not be any brother or sister who is in need (Acts 4:32-35)

- We have forgotten that we are all to be one in thought in the body of Christ, without division (1 Corinthians 1:10), and that our division shows our lack of spiritual maturity (1 Corinthians 3:3)
- We have forgotten that our goal should be to all attain the same level of spiritual maturity in Christ (1 Peter 3:8)

How can it be that less than 9% of Christians want to get together outside of Sunday services for even an hour one day a week where they can study God's Word together and get to know their brothers and sisters better? (5)

Because the people of the church have forgotten who God is, who we are in relation to God, and who we are in relation to each other, we have also forgotten what our purpose is on the earth –

- We have forgotten that we were called to follow in Jesus' footsteps (1 Peter 2:21), to seek and save the lost (Luke 19:10), and to serve God the Father in humility as Jesus did (Philippians 2:5-8)
- We have forgotten that we are citizens of heaven (Philippians 3:20), we are strangers and pilgrims on earth (Hebrews 11:13), and not part of this world (John 17:16)
- We have forgotten that we are ambassadors of Christ on this earth and that God makes His appeal to the lost through us (2 Corinthians 5:17-20)
- We have forgotten that we are not to live our lives for ourselves, but for the will of God (1 Peter 4:2)
- We have forgotten that we are to be holy because the Lord is holy (1 Peter 1:15), and that anyone who names the name of the Lord should depart from wickedness (2 Timothy 2:17)
- We have forgotten that we are to grow in knowledge of the Lord (2 Peter 3:18), because we are to be imitators of God (Ephesians 5:1)

Introduction

- We have forgotten that we have been chosen to go and bear good fruit (John 15:16), and that our good works were prepared by God before we were born (Ephesians 2:10)
- We have forgotten that we are to use the money that God gives us to share with others in the church, as this is a very powerful testimony to the world, and it brings much glory to God (2 Corinthians 9:5-14)

How can it be that less than one third of Christians have shared their faith with a nonbeliever in the last six months? (6) How can it be that the main goals in life of Christians differ very little from those of nonbelievers? (7) How can it be that 9 out of 10 pastors will not instruct their congregations on what God's Word says regarding political policies and political candidates when Christians are commanded to discern and elect godly leaders? (8) How can it be that only half of all pastors have a biblical worldview (9), and only 10% of Christians say they have a biblical worldview? (10) How can it be that most Christians give less than 3% of their income back to God and His kingdom work? (11)

The people of the church have forgotten who God is, who we are in relation to God, who we are in relation to the world and what our purpose is on the earth because we do not spend enough time reading God's Word, the Bible. Nearly forty percent of Christians do not read the Bible over the course of a week, and only one out of four Christians has read the entire Bible. (12)

We must read God's Word daily because -

- God's Word was written by God (2 Peter 1:20-21)
- God's Word will be fulfilled completely (Ezekiel 12:28)
- God's Word tells us the end from the beginning (Isaiah 46:9-10)
- God's Word was made certain by the resurrection of Jesus (2 Peter 1:16-19)
- God's Word says all knowledge is found in Christ (Colossians 2:3)

- God's Word says knowledge of Christ leads to eternal life and godliness (2 Peter 1:3)
- God's Word is useful for teaching, rebuking and training in righteousness (2 Timothy 3:16)
- We are purified by obeying the truth found in God's Word (1 Peter 1:22)
- We are to be doers of God's Word (James 1:22)
- We are to crave God's Word like newborns crave milk (1 Peter 2:2), because only one thing is needed, to listen to God's Word (Luke 10:41-42)

Ultimately, the people of the church have forgotten who God is, who they are in relation to God, who they are in relation to each other, what their purpose is on the earth, and do not spend enough time reading God's Word the Bible, because they do not fear God (see chapter two for what it means to 'fear' the Lord God) –

- We should fear the Lord because He spoke everything into existence –

"Let all the earth fear the Lord; let all inhabitants of the world stand in awe of Him. For He spoke, and it was done; He commanded, and it stood fast." – Psalm 33:8-9

- We should fear God because His judgement is coming –

"Fear God and give glory to Him, for the hour of his judgement has come; and worship Him who made heaven and earth, the sea and springs of water." – Revelation 14:7

- We should fear the Lord because He will watch over us and deliver our souls –

"Behold, the eye of the Lord is on those who fear Him, on those who hope in His mercy, to deliver their soul from death…" – Psalm 33:18-19

- We should fear God because He has the power to cast into hell –

Introduction

"Do not be afraid of those who kill the body, and after that have no more they can do. But I will show you whom you should fear; fear Him who after He has killed, has power to cast into hell. Yes, I say to you, fear Him!" – Luke 12:4-5

- We should fear the Lord because it moves us away from evil –

"By the fear of the Lord one departs from evil." – Proverbs 16:6

- We should fear of the Lord and depart from evil because it will bring health to the body –

"Fear the Lord and depart from evil. It will be health to your flesh and strength to your bones." – Proverbs 3:7-8

- We should spend our time on earth in fear of God –

"Conduct yourselves throughout the time of your stay here in fear." – 1 Peter 1:17

- We should serve God in reverent fear –

"Let us have grace, by which we may serve God acceptably with reverence and godly fear." – Hebrews 12:28

- Fear of the Lord brings wisdom and understanding –

"The fear of the Lord is the beginning of wisdom, and the knowledge of the Holy One is understanding." – Proverbs 9:10

- We should fear God because judgment will begin with the church, and even with His saving grace, we are barely saved –

"For it is time for judgment to begin at the household of God...And if the righteous is scarcely saved, what will become of the ungodly and the sinner?" – 1 Peter 4:17-18

There are many reasons to fear God, but probably the most important one is because God's Word says it is possible, through persistent willful disobedience to His Word, for God to consider it unbelief. And since salvation is by God's grace, through faith (belief), it would follow that that would mean it is possible for a believer to lose their salvation due to a certain amount of willful, persistent disobedience. What or where that point is that God would consider willful disobedience to be unbelief (no matter what we profess) I do not know; but we will devote an entire chapter to this topic at the end of the book because of its importance.

For those who may be tempted to put the book down at this point because you think that losing one's salvation is heresy, I would like to point out that there are basically three verses in the Bible that once saved always saved proponents like to quote to back up their belief that a believer can never lose their salvation, but they always take those verses out of context and do not interpret them against the rest of God's Word. I will show you over fifty verses from the Bible that seem to indicate a believer can lose their salvation, and would also add that there are two entire books in the New Testament that were written as warnings to their hearers that it is possible to willfully disobey God to the point of losing our salvation – Galatians and Hebrews.

If you want to skip to the last chapter and read it first because you just cannot continue without hearing that argument, be my guest. But for now, we are going to continue with the first of the twelve steps to hearing, "Well done, good and faithful servant," when you meet Jesus for the first time. These steps are not in an exact order, although the first two are absolutely necessary and must precede the others; otherwise trying to do the remaining steps will prove impossible. However, the steps listed after the first two are set up in a way that could help serve as an indication of one's spiritual growth in their faith; in order to kind of give you an idea of where you might be in that regard.

Chapter 1

One Must Be a True Believer

The first step that is absolutely necessary to hearing, "Well done, good and faithful servant," when someone meets Jesus for the first time is that person must be a true believer according to God's Word. There are only two positions a person can be before God, under His saving grace (Ephesians 2:8) or under His wrath (Ephesians 2:1-4). Jesus, who is God (John 14:9), confirms this when He said we are either for Him or against Him (Luke 11:23). There are no positions before God other than these two.

For those who are under God's saving grace through faith in Jesus, they are for Him, because God has sent His Holy Spirit to reside in that person (John 14:15-17); and through the Holy Spirit living inside them they can call Jesus their Lord and Savior. No one can truthfully call Jesus their Lord unless God's Holy Spirit is living inside them (1 Corinthians 12:3), inside their heart (2 Corinthians 1:22). For everyone else who is not under God's saving grace through faith in Jesus, they are against Him, and under God's wrath (Romans 1:18).

Now there are a couple things that need to be pointed out here. Some things that even those who are part of God's eklessia, the church, don't like to hear. The first is that God's Word says most people are under His wrath, and most people will die in that condition and will spend eternity in punishment. That is not a popular teaching and my guess would be you haven't heard a sermon about that in a long time, or possibly never have, but that is what God's Word says.

In Matthew, chapter seven, Jesus talks about the road to destruction (eternal punishment) being broad, and the gate to eternal destruction being wide, and many will enter through it (verse 13). In contrast, Jesus says the gate to life (eternal life in heaven) is narrow, and the road difficult, and there are few who find it (verse 14). There is no way to interpret these verses other than the majority of people who have lived, and will live on the earth, have not and will not choose to be under God's saving grace through faith, and will go through the gate to eternal punishment.

The second thing that most people don't like to hear, including those in the church, is that the eternal punishment Jesus is talking about is much worse than most people think. Many pastors, when they talk about eternal punishment call it 'eternal separation from God,' and while that is a true statement, it doesn't come close to describing what really happens. The punishment Jesus is talking about is spending an eternity of suffering in a lake of fire (Revelation 20:15) that was originally prepared for the devil and all the other angels that also rebelled against God (Matthew 25:41).

That is the final place where every person will go that has not accepted God's saving grace through faith. This is a very sad thought, but true according to God's Word; and I'm sure it's one of the reasons Jesus was called among His many names in the Bible, a man of sorrows (Isaiah 53:3). Jesus knew that even though He came, was going to die on the cross and be raised to life to defeat sin and death in order to provide a way for people to avoid the lake of fire, most people were going to reject what He did for them, and would end up in the lake of fire for all eternity.

That thought makes it hard for me, at times, to go through life with an outward expression of joy (although inward I always have joy in God my Savior) because everywhere I go, I see many people over the age of accountability* and know the majority will reject what Jesus did for each of them, and they will end up in that lake of fire.

Now while I confess this knowledge makes it hard for me at times to keep a smile on my face, it is also something that drives me to serve God in ways that all true believers are all called to do. We are called to share the hope we have of our eternal salvation with those God has put around us (1 Peter 3:15), so that we might be the instrument God uses to save some of them (2 Corinthians 5:20). We are called to be holy because God is holy (1 Peter 1:15-16), to live a life filled with good works (Titus 3:8), and to love others in the same way that Jesus loves us (John 13:34), even to the point of death (John 15:13). Not coincidentally, these are all things

Chapter 1: One Must Be a True Believer

that are part of the steps to hearing, "Well done, good and faithful servant," but it must begin with being a true believer.

So how do we make sure we are on the right road and will pass through the narrow gate to eternal life? What does God's Word say?

The Bible says we must hear (or read) the gospel, also known as the good news (1 Corinthians 15:3-4), which says we are under God's wrath because of our sins against Him and that without some way of forgiveness we will spend an eternity in punishment. And that Jesus provided the only means for forgiveness by being crucified for our sins and raised to life for our justification that we might be saved (Romans 4:25). This hearing or reading of the gospel must produce faith (Hebrews 4:2), for we must come to God through faith in Jesus (John 14:6). This faith must be in the real Jesus of the Bible, not a fake or made-up Jesus (John 8:24).

Once the hearing of the gospel produces faith in us, we receive God's Holy Spirit (Ephesians 1:13) and we confess with our mouth that Jesus is Lord and believe in our hearts that God raised Jesus from the dead (Romans 10:9-10). Then we are saved and have peace with God (Romans 5:1), not being under His wrath anymore (1 Thessalonians 5:9), but are considered children of God (Romans 8:16). Let's take a look at each one of those in a little more detail.

First of all, I would like to point out that children under a certain age can be saved without hearing the gospel.* We have this recorded in God's Word when king David's newborn son died and David said he would go to see his son someday in heaven, but his son would not return to him (2 Samuel 12:23). Obviously, his son did not hear the gospel (Jesus wasn't going to come and reveal the gospel for another thousand years) but he was saved anyway and the only way to account for this is children under a certain age are not held accountable for their sins.

Some of you may say he was only a newborn and did not sin so that is why he was saved. But God's Word says we are all sinful from the womb (Psalm 51:5), because sin has been handed down from the time of Adam through the father (Romans 5:12), causing everyone to be born with a sinful nature (Romans 7:18). For this reason, Jesus was conceived inside the virgin Mary through the Holy Spirit, making God Jesus' Father (Luke 1:35), and making Jesus both divine (God incarnate) and the only human ever born without sin (Hebrews 7:26). However, for everyone else born with a sinful nature and over the age of accountability for their sins, they must hear the gospel because saving faith comes by hearing or reading the gospel found in God's Word (Romans 10:17).

The message of the gospel is in two parts, and it must contain both parts or it is not the gospel. The first part of the gospel says that everyone has sinned and fallen short of the glory of God (Romans 3:23), and because we have sinned against God we will die (Romans 6:23) and come under judgment for our sins (Hebrews 9:27). An eternal and holy God (Isaiah 43:10-11, Revelation 4:8) must punish sin (2 Peter 2:4-6), and since our souls are eternal (Ecclesiastes 12:7), our eternal souls must be punished eternally (Matthew 25:46); which we've already seen is an eternity in the lake of fire. Without some way of forgiveness for our sins this would be the fate of each and every one of us. That is the first part of the gospel and hearing it should bring us to a point of conviction before God for our sins.

This conviction, or acknowledgement of our sins, should then lead to repentance. Repentance is a word that in Biblical context means to turn away from sin. We must repent and turn away from our sins (Acts 17:30). Not only because Jesus said we must repent to be saved (Luke 13:3), and repentance is a necessary step that leads to saving faith (2 Corinthians 7:10), but also because without turning from sin it will not be possible to do the next step after becoming a true believer, which is to get sin out of our lives. How can we get sin out of our lives if we do not turn from it?

The second part of the gospel is what God did to provide the way for the forgiveness of sins. God became flesh in the person of Jesus Christ (Philippians 2:6-7), lived the perfect life that none of us could live (Hebrews 4:15), to become the perfect sacrifice for our sins (Hebrews 7:27) once and for all time (Hebrews 10:12). He let His own creation kill Him (John 10:18) on a cross for our sins and was raised to life three days later (Matthew 28:6-7), so that those who believe in what He did for them could not only be alive again now (Colossians 2:13), but also inherit eternal life with Him (John 3:16). That's the good news of the gospel. God did this for you and for me, it was personal (Galatians 2:20); done out of His love for us that is outside the realm of human understanding (Ephesians 3:19).

When someone hears or reads that gospel, the hearing or reading must produce faith in that person (Hebrews 4:2), because it is only through faith that we are saved (Ephesians 2:8-9). This has been the case since even before Jesus came (Hebrews 11). Faith in God has always been the method through which a person is saved from eternal punishment, and it is also a requirement for anyone who wants to please God (Hebrews 11:6). This is why a person who wants to hear, 'Well done, good and faithful servant,' cannot skip the first step of faith. He or she must have faith, not only to be a true believer, but they also must have faith for anything they do throughout their lives to be pleasing to God.

Now *who* a person has faith in for their salvation is extremely important. Jesus said unless you believe He is who He says He is, you will die in your sins (John 8:24), and that would mean eternal punishment in the lake of fire. We cannot come to God any other way than through Jesus (John 14:6), so believing who Jesus says He is, the Son of God (Luke 22:70), God Himself (John 10:30), and the resurrected Christ who defeated death (Revelation 1:18) is essential to one being a true believer, and essential to one's salvation (1 Corinthians 15:13-17).

When a person believes in the Jesus from God's Word, the Bible says God sends His Holy Spirit to live in that person (John 14:15-17), inside their heart (Romans 5:5). This indwelling of God's Holy Spirit serves many purposes. It makes that person alive spiritually (John 6:63), which is a big deal because for all those that do not have the Holy Spirit inside of them, God considers them walking dead people (Matthew 8:22). The Spirit living inside a person allows them to be born again (1 Peter 1:22-23), which is a requirement for getting into heaven (John 3:3). It also allows that person to be called a child of God (Romans 8:14-17), and for them to be able to call God their Father, even call Him 'Daddy' (verse 15). The Holy Spirit living inside a person allows them to become heirs with Christ (verse 17), heirs to the kingdom of God (James 2:5), and the Spirit will teach that person the things of God (1 Corinthians 2:10).

However, the most important purpose of the Holy Spirit living inside someone is it identifies that person as one who has been redeemed (their sins forgiven) by the crucified and risen Lord Jesus Christ (Galatians 3:13-14). God's Word says Jesus *also* lives in a person's heart through the indwelling of the Holy Spirit (Galatians 4:6). And if a person does not have Christ living in them, they are not His (Romans 8:9); and if they are not His, they are not saved (John 3:36). So you can see, the indwelling of the Holy Spirit is something that is critically important, not only for a person's salvation, but also as we will see later on, for carrying out the remaining steps. Once a person has received the Holy Spirit through faith in Jesus, that person has peace with God (Romans 5:1), and is no longer under God's wrath (Romans 5:9), but rather God calls that person a child of God (John 1:12) and a friend (John 15:14-15).

Sounds easy enough, right? Receive what God did for you through faith in Jesus; His life, death and resurrection and you will be saved? Well, it is easy, but also it isn't.

It's easy because God did all the work necessary for saving grace through faith and all we have to do is receive that free gift (Romans 5:15-18), but it also isn't easy because everyone has a sinful nature that doesn't want the Holy Spirit living inside them (Romans 8:7, NIV), because there is nothing good about the sinful flesh (Romans 7:18). So, when God's Spirit is living inside a person, there is a battle raging between the sinful flesh and the Spirit (Galatians 5:17-18 NLT) as He works to transform us into someone who is more like Christ (Ephesians 4:15). This battle that goes on inside every true believer is the reason why we must submit to the Holy Spirit inside us and He will cleanse us from the inside out from sin (Galatians 5:22-25).

Now this would be a good time to stop for a minute and ask a question. I'm assuming most people who read this book are either true believers who genuinely want to hear, 'Well done good and faithful servant,' and are reading it for that reason; or are true believers who have been on the sidelines for a while and the Holy Spirit has directed you to this book to 'get going' in fulfilling what God has prepared in advance for you to do (Ephesians 2:10). Either way, that's great and is one of the reasons this book was written.

So, the question I'm going to ask is for all true believers reading this book, but it is also helpful for those who may not be so sure if they have

Chapter 1: One Must Be a True Believer

truly received God's grace through faith in Jesus and have the Holy Spirit living inside them.

Do you feel the battle going on inside your flesh between your sinful nature and God's Holy Spirit?

If you answered yes, that's great. That is one indication you have passed the test that God's Word says every believer should give themselves to make sure they are 'in the faith' (2 Corinthians 13:5). If you answered no, or you're not sure, then the advice I would give to you is the same the apostle Paul gave to the believers at the church in Corinth – Test yourself to see if you are in the faith.

So how do we test ourselves? God's Word says we can test ourselves through our actions, or works as the Bible calls them (James 2:18); and is probably one of the main reasons the apostle Paul was always writing in his letters to the churches to make sure the believers were doing lots of good works (Romans 13:3, Ephesians 2:10, 1 Timothy 5:9-10, 24-25, 6:18, Titus 2:7, 2:14, 3:8, 3:14. If the believers in the churches were doing a lot of good works, they were proving their faith. Another part of God's Word calls it doing acts befitting repentance (Acts 26:20). Repentance is a necessary step in coming to faith in Christ (2 Corinthians 7:10), so if a believer is doing good works because they have turned from their sin, they can be sure Jesus is living inside them, and they are in the faith.

Before we move on to the next chapter, I want to point something out that I will cover in an entire section at the end of the book, but it needs to be mentioned here. This test that believers are to give themselves is not a one and done kind of test, it should be done constantly over the course of their lives. God's Word is very clear that we can move away from the good works we used to do at first (Revelation 2:4-5), and Jesus does not like it when we do that because it's an indication that our love for Him has faded (verse 4). God's Word is also clear that if believers continue to live a life that looks more like rebellion against God than belief in Him (no matter what we may profess with our mouth), it is our actions that truly tell where our hearts lie (Isaiah 29:13, Titus 1:16). God will consider constant willful rebellion unbelief (Hebrews 3:12-19), and that is a very dangerous place to be.

If we are saved through faith (belief) in Jesus, but God considers someone to be in a state of unbelief because of their actions, is that person truly saved? For those of you that can't wait to get that question answered, chapter twelve lays out the argument, according to God's Word, that they are not. And that one can go from being saved under God's grace to choosing not be under it anymore through constant gratification of the sinful nature, which is rebellion against God.

Skipping to chapter twelve and coming back to chapter two will not interrupt the flow of the book. The last chapter stands on its own as a warning to those who think they can mock God by claiming Christ as their Savior but then living their lives anyway they want (Galatians 6:7). It doesn't work that way. If more believers understood that, there would be a lot more fear of God in the church than there is; and the church would also have a lot more power and impact on the world than it does right now.

But as the apostle Paul would say, I have confidence that that is not the case with you dear reader (2 Thessalonians 3:4). So, let's take a look at the next step to hearing, 'Well done, good and faithful servant,' when you meet Jesus for the first time.

Chapter 2

One Must Turn From Their Sin

The next step after a person becomes a true believer in Christ is they must begin to get sin out of their life. This is not easy, as the sinful nature, also referred to as the flesh in the Bible (Romans 7:18, NASB), doesn't just roll over and die once a person becomes a Christian (Galatians 5:17). On the contrary, it fights harder than ever to keep that person entangled in the life of habitual sin that the flesh has enjoyed and doesn't want to give up (1 Peter 2:11).

Yes, there are places in God's Word that say all true believers have been crucified with Christ (Galatians 2:20), that they have died with Christ (Colossians 3:3) and that they now live a new life in Him (2 Corinthians 5:17) and for Him (2 Corinthians 5:15). However, there are also Scriptures that say our sinful nature will always be with us this side of heaven (Romans 7:21), and even though we are called to live godly lives once we proclaim the name of Jesus as Lord and Savior (1 Peter 1:15), the battle that will go on inside the members of our body over sin will be anything but easy (Romans 7:22-24).

Despite this difficulty, God's Word says we are to turn from our sins (repent) which means we need to recognize we are sinners before a holy God and turn from sin. Then, once we receive His saving grace though faith in Jesus, we must stop sinning willfully, because that is not who we are anymore (1 John 5:18). Once a person has turned from their sins and received God's Holy Spirit and is saved, that person has become a citizen of heaven (Philippians 3:20). That is their present state now (Ephesians 2:6), not just something they become after they die. In addition, not only are they citizens of heaven now, serving as ambassadors from heaven to this world (2 Corinthians 5:20), but they are expected to live as ones looking forward to returning to their heavenly realm someday (Hebrews 13:14).

Believers are expected to do this because when a person dies to their sinful nature (Romans 6:2) and is made alive again through the indwelling of the Holy Spirit (John 6:63), they become espoused to be married to Christ (2 Corinthians 11:2, KJV). This is done according to the Jewish process of marriage at the time when Jesus came. A man would first pay a price to the father of the woman that he wanted to marry. They would then draw up a contract for the marriage and the man went away to prepare a place at his father's house for his bride to be. The bride busied herself getting ready for the bridegroom to return and take her to their new home, but she was not told when that would happen. It was up to the father of the bridegroom to decide when the time was right for his son to go get his bride.

Throughout the wait, the bride agreed in the contract to keep herself pure and undefiled for the bridegroom, and he promised to come back and get her when his father told him it was time. The bride would light a lamp every night in hope that the bridegroom would return, and also to let the entire town know she was espoused. That's important because the bridegroom usually would come at night to make sure she was being faithful to their marriage contract by keeping her lamp lit. The father of the bridegroom would then announce to his son with trumpets that it was time to go get his bride, and as he went to get her, it was announced with shouting as he approached. If she had been faithful while she was waiting, he took her back to his father's house where they were formally married and spent one week together before the wedding party began. After the wedding party was over, they spent the rest of their lives living there, in the presence of the bridegroom's father.

Let's see how this applies to God's saving grace.

Jesus is the bridegroom (Luke 5:33-35) and all true believers in the church are the bride (Ephesians 5:25). Jesus paid the price required by God the Father for the bride by being killed on the cross for them (Colossians 1:19-20). After being raised from the dead (1 Corinthians 15:20-23), a marriage contract was drawn up (The New Testament) and

Chapter 2: One Must Turn From Their Sin

Jesus went back to His Father's house in heaven to prepare a place for His bride (John 14:2-3).

When the time comes, which is already set (Acts 17:31), God the Father will tell His Son Jesus to go get His bride. It will be announced from heaven with a trumpet blast and a shout (1 Thessalonians 4:16). All true believers who have died will be resurrected first, then all true believers still alive will be changed into their resurrected bodies in the blink of an eye (1 Corinthians 15:52, NLT). They will all be taken out of this world to meet Jesus in the clouds and He will take them all back to heaven with Him (1 Thessalonians 4:17).

They will stay there together for seven years (one year for each of the seven days) while God the Father pours out His wrath on an unbelieving world (Revelation chapters 6-18). At the end of those seven years, Jesus will return with His bride (Revelation 19:11-14) and raise up those who died in faith in Him during the last seven years (Revelation 20:4). He will then set up His kingdom on earth for a thousand years (verse 4), which is the wedding party, and it will all lead into an eternity of being with Jesus in the presence of God the Father (Revelation 21:3).

The model is the same, and this is what is occurring right now between the bridegroom Jesus and all true believers who are espoused to Him. There are two things I didn't mention until now but they are very important. While the bridegroom was away preparing a place for his bride, the contract said they were essentially married at that point, and is the reason all true believers are married to Jesus right now, because that is what our contract says too (Romans 7:4). The other thing to point out is that if the bridegroom comes and finds the bride has broken the marriage contract and not remained faithful to him, he doesn't have to marry her anymore. This is why we need to take our marriage contract seriously. We are to remain faithful and pure while we wait for Jesus to return.

So, how do we do that? Let's go back to the wedding model and look at it from our perspective, as the bride.

God's Word says every true believer is chosen by Jesus (John 15:16). This means Jesus chose you and me to be married to Him. Jesus said to God the Father before you were born (Psalm 139:16), I want this person to be married to Me. This choice was made even before the foundation of the world was made (Ephesians 1:4)! Jesus then came and paid a huge payment to God the Father by being obedient to death on a cross for you (Philippians 2:8).

At the proper time, God the Father sent you to Jesus (John 6:65), meaning you were given the marriage proposal in the form of hearing the gospel (Romans 10:17), and you had the choice to say yes or no. If you repented of your sins and realized your need to be married to the bridegroom Jesus to bring you eternal life (Romans 6:23), you said yes and the marriage contract spoken of in the Old Testament (Genesis 3, Isaiah 53), and fulfilled in the New Testament (John 19:30), now applies to you.

So, what's in the marriage contract that we must do?

- We must realize we are married now, this makes us citizens of heaven now
- We must be in the process of purification (sanctification), which means becoming more like God, like Jesus
- We must understand our calling to be holy
- We must keep our lamps lit in this dark world, to let everyone know we belong to Jesus and to let Jesus know we are waiting faithfully for Him to return
- We must submit to our husband Jesus. This is done by submitting to the Holy Spirit inside us
- We must take the contract seriously by fearing God, because if we don't stay faithful and pure until Jesus returns, we can miss the wedding

Let's take a look at those one at a time, understanding that each one of those six points is also a reason we need to get sin out of our lives.

God's Word says that when a man marries a woman, the two become one flesh (Genesis 2:24), and it is no different with our marriage to Jesus (Ephesians 5:31-32). The Bible says we are one with Jesus, part of His flesh and bones (Ephesians 5:30), and with the life that we have been given through the indwelling of the Holy Spirit (Titus 3:5-6), this makes us present with Him in heaven right now (Ephesians 2:6). All true believers are citizens of heaven now (Philippians 3:20), we are not citizens of this world. Jesus said He is not part of this world, and anyone married to Him is not part of this world either (John 17:14). If anyone married to Christ is not part of this world, then their conduct should reflect their heavenly citizenship. Since citizens of this world live according to the sinful nature (2 Peter 1:3-4, NIV), we must do the opposite and get sin out of our lives (Ephesians 4:17-24).

God's Word says that while the bridegroom is away preparing a place for us, we need to be in the process of purifying ourselves in preparation for Jesus' return (Romans 6:11-14, 2 Corinthians 11:2). This process is called sanctification (Romans 6:19, NASB), which means becoming more like Christ; rather than who we used to be when we lived according to the sinful desires of the flesh (Colossians 3:1-10). This process takes time and will never be fully completed in a believer's lifetime, either before their body dies or Jesus returns, because it is not possible to be completely like Jesus until we are made like Him when He appears again (1 John 3:2). Nevertheless, becoming more like Jesus in this life means we must get sin out of our lives.

Once we are espoused to Christ, our marriage contract calls us to be holy (1 Peter 1:15-16), because the Son of God, our Bridegroom, who is God in the flesh (John 1:14), is holy (Hebrews 7:26). This may be considered to be the same thing as sanctification, and it is to some extent. However, in the same way that the One True God exists in three persons - in God the Father, in the person of Jesus Christ, and in the Holy Spirit (1 John 5:7) - we are being called to be holy by each of those three persons who make up the Triune God, and that shouldn't be missed.

We are called by God the Father to be holy in places like 1 Thessalonians 4:7-8 and James 1:16-25. We are called by Jesus to be holy in places like 1 Peter 1:15-16 and 2:24. We are called by the Holy Spirit to be holy in places like Romans 8:1-13 and Galatians 5:16-17, and these are only a few examples of many from God's Word. Yes, our marriage contract is written in relation to the bridegroom Jesus, but since God the Father, God the Son, and God the Holy Spirit are one God (Matthew

28:19), they all call us to be holy at the same time. This should serve as an indication of how important it is to God that we be holy and get sin out of our lives.

We also must keep our lamps lit while He is away preparing a place for us (Matthew 5:14-16). This is done for the same reasons the bride would light her lamp each night until the groom returned. First and foremost, she wanted to show everyone that she was espoused, essentially married to another already, and that she was not available to be married to anyone else. As true believers in Jesus, we need to show the world that we are His (1 Corinthians 6:19-20), and we do this by being a light in the darkness of this world (Philippians 2:15).

There are many other places in God's Word that compare a believer's life and what it represents in this world to being a light (Luke 11:33-36, 16:8, John 3:21, 12:36, Acts 13:47, Romans 2:19, Ephesians 5:8, 1 Thessalonians 5:5, 1 John 1:7). Those comparisons talk about being a shining light through the doing of good things (Matthew 5:16, 12:35, Mark 9:50, Luke 6:35, Romans 12:21, Galatians 6:9-10, Ephesians 2:10, 1 Timothy 6:18, Titus 3:14), not doing sinful things, so we must get sin out of our lives if we want to keep our lamp shining.

Also, the lamp was lit in hopeful expectation that the groom would return that night to bring her home. As a believer in Jesus, do you ever pray "Come, Lord Jesus" and mean it? I hope you do, but do you realize what it means to pray that prayer? If you are married, have kids, a house, cars, and whatever else you may consider something of important value, when the bridegroom Jesus comes, you will lose it all for Him (Philippians 3:7-9, 1 Timothy 6:7). Do you realize that?

If your spouse or kids are believers too, or your kids are under the age of accountability, they will be saved with you when Jesus comes.* So, it doesn't mean that you won't be able to be with them in heaven. However, it does mean you will not be married to your spouse anymore (Luke 20:34-35), and your kids will not be your kids anymore in an earthly sense. They will be more like all your other brothers and sisters, sharing in everything that belongs to Christ (Hebrews 3:14, NLT); because at that point, we will all be glorified heirs and rulers with Him (Romans 8:16-17).

Chapter 2: One Must Turn From Their Sin

Does this change your mind about praying that prayer? I hope it does not, because Jesus said anyone who loves his husband or wife or kids more than Him is not worthy of being married to Him (Matthew 10:37). He also said anyone who loves the life they have in this world more than Him cannot be married to Him (Luke 9:24, John 12:25). We *must* put the hopeful expectation of our bridegroom Jesus coming at any time (Titus 2:13), and being ready for it, at the top of our list of priorities (1 Thessalonians 5:1-6).

Now this doesn't mean we neglect everything else. On the contrary, getting our priorities straight should help our marriages and relationships with our kids because it will allow us to love them with the love of Christ (Philippians 2:1-4). This will far surpass any effort we could do to love them apart from Him. But we cannot build our foundation on the Rock, on our bridegroom Jesus as He tells us to do (Luke 6:47-48), unless we put the priority of fulfilling our marriage contract to Him first.

We already mentioned that these marriage contracts also said when the groom was away preparing a place for him and his bride to be, they were considered already married during that time. This means everything that God's Word says about a husband and wife, and how they should live in relation to one another, applies right now to all true believers in their relation to their bridegroom Jesus. So, what does the Bible say? Well, it says a lot, and I would suggest you read up on it in places like 1 Corinthians chapter 7 and Ephesians chapter 5, but the main thing to point out here is that not only are spouses supposed to submit to each other in Christ (Ephesians 5:21), but since Jesus is our spouse, we should be very careful to submit to Him in every way that our marriage contract says we are to do (verse 22).

Jesus once asked the question, *"Why do you call Me Lord but do not do what I say?"* (Luke 6:46). In the context of our marriage contract to Him, He is saying why do you call me your Bridegroom but do not submit to Me as my wife? It's a great question, and something that we must do; but this can only truly be done by submitting to the Holy Spirit living inside of us; because only through the Holy Spirit can we understand our marriage contract found in God's Word (1 Corinthians 2:10-14).

We already learned that the sinful nature does not go away when a person becomes a believer in Christ, and that it will fight to keep things the way they were. Even going so far as to war against the soul (1 Peter 2:11). The sinful nature is hostile to God and cannot submit to Him (Romans 8:7), so we cannot submit to our bridegroom Jesus any other way than by making a choice to submit to the Holy Spirit. And make no mistake, it is a choice. The apostle Paul tells believers many times to do this or to do that through the Spirit (Romans 7:6, 15:13, 30, Galatians 5:16, 22-23, 6:8, Ephesians 2:18, 3:16, 6:17-18, 2 Timothy 1:14). However, Paul also tells us not to grieve the Holy Spirit (Ephesians 4:30), nor quench the Spirit (1 Thessalonians 5:19). So we do have the choice to do one or the other; to submit to the Holy Spirit or not to submit to Him.

Jesus confirms this when He talks about knocking on the door of the hearts of people who are already believers (Revelation 3:20). Jesus is saying let Me in to your heart (submit to My Spirit living inside you) and I will 'dine with you'. There is no better place to strengthen a relationship than when you are eating a meal and sharing conversation with another person. So it should be no surprise that Jesus says if we open our hearts to Him, He will come in and share a meal with us. However, this submission, this opening of the door of your heart to the bridegroom Jesus, can only be done by first submitting to God's Holy Spirit living inside you (1 Corinthians 12:3). Then, by continuing to submit to the Holy Spirit, He will help you get sin out of your life and present you as a faithful bride to the Bridegroom when He comes (2 Corinthians 11:2).

Last, but certainly not least, as the bride of Christ we need to have a healthy fear of the Lord. This will help us stay motivated to continually submit to the Holy Spirit in order to fulfill our part of the marriage contract and get sin out of our lives. Fear in this context is both a combination of reverence and awe because of the Lord's power, might and righteousness. But Jesus also says we are to fear Him because He is a just God; One who can send both body and soul to hell (Matthew 10:28).

For reverence and awe there are verses from God's Word like He sees everything everywhere (Hebrews 4:13), and there is no place a person can go where the Lord does not see them (Jeremiah 23:24). This also means that the Lord will be able to bring every deed into judgment, whether good or evil (Ecclesiastes 12:14). Now that sounds bad, but when you combine it all with the fact that those that are under God's saving grace will not be dealt with according to their sins (Psalm 103:10), nor punished for their iniquities (Romans 8:1), then the reverence and awe for His mercy becomes clear as well.

However, there are many more applications in God's Word for the other kind of fear of the Lord, the traditional sense of the word fear, that are not talked about as much. It's a shame that the church has gotten away from that kind of preaching because the first and second Great Awakenings in the church relied upon that kind of instruction to motivate people to get sin out of their lives (and they did, which is why those periods are singled out, not only in the history of the church, but of the world).

God's Word also says to fear the Lord is to turn from evil (Proverbs 3:7), to hate evil behavior, pride, arrogance and perverse speech (Proverbs 8:13); to hate *everything* that is evil and to cling to what is good (Romans 12:9). The Bible also says that God is against those who practice evil (2 Peter 3:12), that we are not to share in the sins of others (1 Timothy 5:22), and that those who indulge the sinful nature will be judged for punishment (2 Peter 2:10).

As the bride of Christ, we have seen that it is in our contract that we must remain faithful and pure to the Bridegroom until He returns to bring us home. If we are not doing that because we are constantly living in sin rather than getting it out of our lives, does Jesus still have to take us as His bride when He comes or if we go to Him through death? God's Word says if we say we know the bridegroom Jesus, but continue living in sin we lie (1 John 1:6-7); and that no one who habitually sins knows the bridegroom Jesus...but is of the devil (1 John 3:6-10)! Those are very strong words that seem to indicate Jesus does not have to take a bride when He returns who has not remained faithful to Him.

Jesus taught this in a parable from Matthew chapter 25. He said there were ten virgins espoused to be married to a bridegroom, five of them were wise and five of them were foolish (verse 2). The groom went away for a long time (to prepare a place for his brides) and while he was away all ten brides fell asleep (verse 5). When the groom returned and the brides woke up, they were supposed to go out to meet him, but none of them had prepared their lamps. Five of them were able to light their lamps in time, but the other five were not prepared and were not able to light their lamps. As a result, those five were not allowed to go with the groom to the wedding banquet (verse 11).

Now the first thing to point out is that this parable can only be referring to Jesus as the Bridegroom, because God's Word says that on earth, all men are only to be married to one wife (Genesis 2:24), even kings (Deuteronomy 17:17). So, this parable can only be talking about our heavenly marriage to Jesus; and can only be referring to Him when He comes again. Another thing that needs to be understood is that while there are passages in Scripture that talk about how Christians are a shining light in this dark world, the lamps referred to in this parable are a symbol of a person having the Holy Spirit with them. God's Word says if a person does not have Jesus living inside them through the Holy Spirit, they are not Christ's (Romans 8:9). So, the five virgins that were left behind obviously did not have the Holy Spirit (did not have their lamps lit), and were not allowed into heaven to be wed to Jesus for all eternity.

We will come back to this in the last chapter of the book that goes over why a believer in Christ cannot mock the Bridegroom, thinking they can live their life any way they want while they are espoused to Jesus and He will still take them to heaven in marriage when He comes again (Galatians 6:7). There is also something else that should be explained from the parable. This will lead us into the next step to hearing, 'Well done, good and faithful servant,' and it's concerning God's Word itself. We simply must make it a habit to study the Bible.

Chapter 3

Know The Master and His Business

We left off the last chapter with the parable of the Bridegroom coming to get His brides, and acknowledged that in this parable Jesus was talking about Himself, because He is the only one who could possibly be coming to receive more than one bride. Hopefully, you have already picked up your Bible by now and read that parable as it has some helpful information regarding how we are to conduct our lives while we are waiting for the Bridegroom to return.

The parable says all ten brides fell asleep (Matthew 25:5), which means they were not watching for their Bridegroom to return. Since none of them remained awake, this probably means the church as a whole is going to be asleep when Jesus returns. This is not good, and is one of the reasons for me wanting to write this book; in order to try to get some in the church to wake up before He returns. The good news is there is still time for some to wake up and light their lamps, as the parable indicated that half of the brides were able to do so.

However, the bad news is this parable also says there will be a large part of the so called church that will not be prepared when Jesus returns and they will have to go through the Tribulation and prove their faith in Him before they will be able to be His bride. To say they will have to 'go through' the Tribulation is kind of misleading though, as the truth is most of them will have to die for their faith in Jesus.*

Another thing the parable says is that Jesus said the five brides that could not go through the door to be wed to Him were not allowed in because He said He did not know them (25:12). Now there is something very important to point out here and don't miss this. Jesus did not say I *never* knew you to those five brides; He said He didn't know them currently. If He never knew them, they would not have been brides in the first place, and that is a very important difference.

The Bible says Jesus will say to many who try to enter into heaven that He *never* knew them (Matthew 7:23). This means for their entire lives they were separated from Him and never had made the choice to receive God's saving grace through faith in Jesus. Anyone who is in that position would never, at any point, be considered a bride to be wed to Jesus. So, we can be sure that all ten brides in this parable had faith in Jesus at some point in their lives; otherwise not all of them would have been considered to be espoused to Jesus. However, only five *remained* faithful and Jesus took them as brides…because He knew them.

Now if this makes you a bit fearful that it's possible to be considered a bride to be wed to the bridegroom Jesus but when He comes at the Rapture* you will not be taken because He doesn't know you. Then I would say you are probably not doing something that is in your marriage contract to prepare for your wedding to Jesus, and it is this - You must also know your Bridegroom (John 17:3). To illustrate this, let's use the context of a master and his servants.

Jesus is not only our Bridegroom, He is also our Master, and God's Word says we have to do three things in relation to Jesus as our Master –

- We must know our Master
- We need to know our Master's business
- We must live in obedient service to our Master

As a believer in Christ, Jesus is your Master (2 Timothy 2:19-21) and you are His servant (Revelation 1:1). Understanding this relationship is important because servants are supposed to know their master, and their master's business, in order to serve their master effectively. The idea of a servant knowing their master and his business in order to serve him well takes on even more importance for the relationship between a believer and Jesus, because our Master is God (Hebrews 1:8). He expects us to continue His work that He started on earth (John 20:21), and there is no way to do that without knowing Him, because all wisdom and knowledge are found in Christ (Colossians 2:3).

Chapter 3: Know The Master and His Business

So how do we get to know our Master better? Well, our Master is called the Word of God (Revelation 19:13), so it would seem there would be no way to get to know our Master better but by making it a habit to read and study the Bible. Yet, sadly, this is not something that most Christians do. I mentioned earlier that only about 60% of Christians read the Bible even one time in any given week, which means the percentage that read the Bible nearly every day is probably much less. God has revealed Himself and who He is through the person of Jesus Christ (John 14:8-9), and since Jesus is known as the Word of God (John 1:1, 14), Christians simply must make it a goal to read something from the Bible every day, even if it's only a single verse.

Does that sound like too much? Did you know as one of God's chosen people you are commanded to have God's Word in your mind and on your lips from the time you get up in the morning until you go to bed at night? (Deuteronomy 11:18-19). For those Christians that may say well that's the Old Testament, and God was talking to the people of Israel when He said that. No. We are commanded to know both the Old Testament as well as the New Testament (2 Peter 3:2), because it's all God's Word; and all of it is profitable for knowledge, for instruction, for correction, and for training in how to live a righteous life (2 Timothy 3:16).

This sounds like a daunting task, reading, thinking and talking about the Bible daily, but it's not really. Not when you consider everything that God's Word has done, and will continue to do for you.

- Everything you see was created by the Word of God (Hebrews 11:3)

- Knowing God's Word gave you knowledge of Christ that leads to your salvation (2 Timothy 3:15)

- You are sanctified in Christ by the washing of the Word of God (Ephesians 5:26-27)

- Your hope of eternal salvation comes from the Word of God (Psalm 130:5)

- Your offensive weapon against the forces of evil in this world is the sword of the Spirit, which is the Word of God (Ephesians 6:17)
- The Word of God is a double-edged sword, living and active, full of power (Hebrews 4:12)
- If you are constantly studying the truth found in God's Word, you are considered to be of noble character by God (Acts 17:11)

There are so many reasons a believer in Christ should be making it a priority to be reading something from the Bible daily in order to know their Master better.

Did you know –

- Our Master is seated at the right hand of God, with all angels and authorities and powers having been made subject to Him (1 Peter 3:22)
- God has spoken to us through our Master (Hebrews 1:2), and our Master has become for us wisdom from God (1 Corinthians 1:30)
- Our Master is watching us (Hebrews 4:13)
- Our Master will know if our words of worship and praise are genuine or if our hearts are in reality far from Him (Isaiah 29:13)
- Our Master said if we come close to Him, He will come close to us (James 4:8)
- Our Master wants us to be with Him in heaven (John 17:24)
- Our Master will not get discouraged…ever (Isaiah 42:4)

These are just some of the things about our Master that we need to understand in order to know Him better.

Did you know our Master said He declared the end of time from the beginning through His Word? (Isaiah 46:9-10). And what is written in the Bible that has not happened yet is guaranteed to happen in the future, because God's Word is made certain through the resurrection of our Master Jesus Christ from the dead? (2 Peter 1:16-19). God has revealed to us many of the things that are going to happen between now and when

Chapter 3: Know The Master and His Business

our bridegroom Jesus comes at the Rapture; and He has proven they will come true by raising Jesus from the dead. Why wouldn't we want to read the Bible daily to learn more about a Master like that?

Now, not only is it written in our marriage contract that we are we supposed to know our Master so we can be with Him, either when we die or He comes again; but while He is away, we also need to be servants of our Master's business (Colossians 3:17, 23-24). However, to be able to do this we must first know what our Master's business is.

So, what is our Master's business? Well, it's quite simple really. Our Master Jesus is in the business of seeking and saving lost people; this is the reason that He came two thousand years ago (Luke 19:10). Now there certainly are some things that only our Master could do in order to accomplish that such as living the perfect life that no one could live (Hebrews 4:15), to become the perfect sacrifice that God required as payment for sins (9:11-14), so that anyone who would believe in Jesus as their Savior would have eternal life (9:27-28). That is something only our Master Jesus could do, and did (10:9-14).

But there are many other things about our Master's business that certainly are within our power to do as servants called to continue His work (1 Peter 2:9).

- Jesus said He came to call sinners to repentance (Luke 5:32). As repentant sinners, we can let others know that they must repent of their sins (Luke 13:3,5), and turn to the One True God through faith in Jesus for forgiveness of their sins (John 17:3)
- Jesus said He will forgive all those who come to Him through faith (John 6:37), so we must also forgive others as Jesus has already forgiven us (Colossians 3:13)
- Jesus said He came to proclaim the good news of the gospel (Luke 4:18, 43, NIV), to those who were dead in their sins (Ephesians 2:1), so we must always be ready to do the same (1 Peter 3:15, 4:6)
- God (who is our Master) wants all people to be saved (2 Peter 3:9), so we should not consider anyone outside the reach of His saving grace (1 Timothy 1:16)

- Our Master is a defender of the poor and needy (Psalm 140:12, NIV), and says to know Him is to do the same (Jeremiah 22:16), especially for our brothers and sisters (Galatians 6:10)
- Jesus uses us to spread the message of God's saving grace through faith (2 Corinthians 5:18-19). We are His ambassadors to this world and He makes His appeal to others through us (verse 20)
- Our Master's business is made up of many parts (1 Corinthians 12:12), and is compared to a body and how it works together (verses 14-26). Each believer is a part of that body (verse 27), and we have each been given gifts from the Holy Spirit to serve as part of the body of Christ (verses 4-7)

We will talk more about gifts from the Holy Spirit in chapter 9. But for now, these are things that believers need to understand about our Master's business. There are more to be sure, but again, the only way to learn more about our Master and His business is to stay in God's Word every day.

The third thing we have to do in relation with our Master Jesus is we have to live in obedient service to Him. The importance of serving our Master obediently cannot be emphasized enough and will be a continuing theme throughout the rest of this book.

Jesus came as a servant (Matthew 10:28), and He expects us to be servants to Him (John 12:26) and to each other (Galatians 5:13). Jesus wants all His servants to be in unity with each other while they serve Him (Ephesians 4:1-3), because it's a powerful witness to the world that Jesus was sent to save sinners when His believers are in unity (John 17:20-22). This unity between our brothers and sisters is more important to Jesus than even our offerings to Him (Matthew 5:23-24).

God's Word says our Master will discipline those who are not serving Him as they should (Hebrews 12:5-11). It is out of love that He does this (Revelation 3:19), because our Master knows His will for our lives is perfect (Romans 12:2).

Here are some more things that the Bible says regarding the importance of obeying our Master Jesus –

Chapter 3: Know The Master and His Business

- We must put serving our Master at the top of our list of priorities (Luke 9:23-24, 59-62)
- We are to obey the commandments of our Master until He returns again (1 Timothy 6:14)
- We prove we love our Master Jesus by obeying His commands (John 14:21)
- We prove that we know our Master by obeying His commands (1 John 2:3-6)
- Obeying our Master Jesus pleases Him (1 John 3:22)
- Not obeying our Master is considered to be as bad as false religion and idolatry (1 Samuel 15:23, AMP)
- Fearing the Master and obeying His commandments is the whole duty of mankind (Ecclesiastes 12:13)

Jesus takes the obedience of His servants very seriously. Probably the best example of this can be seen from His letters to seven churches in the last book of the Bible, Revelation. There is a lot to be learned from those seven letters, and we will come back to them again at times throughout the book. In the context of being obedient servants though, it is interesting to point out that Jesus had many good things to say about several of the churches, but for most of them, He would follow up all the good things by saying He also had other things against them.

The church at Ephesus had done many good works. They had labored long and hard for Jesus' sake and had not grown weary as they patiently waited for Him. They did not tolerate evil and they hated the doctrine of cheap grace of the Nicolaitans (Revelation 2:2-3), who believed they could live an immoral life because God's grace would save them anyway. Jesus said a couple times in the letters to the seven churches that He hates that doctrine (2:6, 15). Despite all this, Jesus followed up all the good things He had to say about them with what He had against them –that they had left their first love – Him (verse 4).

To the church at Pergamos, Jesus praised them for holding fast to their faith in Him, even though they lived where Satan's throne was (2:13). Yet

He followed up this praise by saying, "I have a few things against you" (2:14). Jesus said they held to the doctrine of Balaam (which is also a form of cheap grace saying believers can lead an immoral life for monetary gain but it will still be ok because of God's grace) and they also had some there practicing the doctrine of the Nicolaitans. Jesus told them to repent from these things, or He would come and fight against them with the sword of His mouth (2:15-16). This sword is the Word of God; the same sword that He will use to strike down the nations and armies opposing Him at the end times. (Revelation 19:15, 21). These are believers Jesus is talking to! Do you think Jesus is ok with these doctrines of cheap grace?

To the church at Thyatira, Jesus praised them for their good works, love, service, faith and patience, and even said they were doing more good works now than before (2:19). Sounds great, right? However, Jesus immediately followed that up by saying He had some things against them; that they tolerate another kind of cheap grace involving sexual immorality called the doctrine of Jezebel (2:20-24). Jesus said if they didn't repent and turn from that teaching that was causing His servants to live an immoral life, He would cast them into great tribulation and He would kill them with death! (verse 22). Do you think Jesus is ok with any doctrine of cheap grace?

All three of these churches had some very positive things they were doing, and Jesus commended them for it; but every time He followed that up with what He had against them. So, we can be sure Jesus takes the obedience of His servants very seriously. And it's a very good reason to make sure we, as believers, are doing all that we can to know our Master Jesus, and His business, so we can remain obedient to Him.

Now if everything you've read in this chapter about knowing our Master Jesus and His business, and being obedient servants to Him, seems like a lot to take in, it is. You will also probably be a little discouraged to know that in this chapter I did not include even half the notes that I took from God's Word regarding these subjects. There is much more that could have been included as well. I can sympathize if you are starting to feel a little overwhelmed at how much there is to learn, and to understand, and to do, in order to hear the words, 'Well done, good and faithful servant,' when you meet Jesus for the first time. But there is hope.

In God's Word we are told how to go about doing everything we are supposed to do in order to accomplish it, and it is this – Live your life as a sacrifice to God.

Well Done, Good and Faithful Servant

Chapter 4

Live Your Life as a Sacrifice to God

At the beginning of the book, I mentioned that the twelve steps to hearing, 'Well done, good and faithful servant,' would not necessarily be presented in an order of doing them from first to last. Although, I did add that you cannot do the last ten without having done steps one and two first. That is still true. However, as the book was coming together, I saw more and more how the twelve steps do seem to fit together in a natural, logical order in the progression of a believer's faith.

Rather than pretend I knew that from the beginning, I think it best that I let the reader know this now, as I believe it lends credibility that the information you are getting is both accurate and necessary to hearing, 'Well done, good and faithful servant,' when you meet Jesus face to face for the first time. So, let's review where we are.

We began the first step with a person must be a true believer and that is because it's impossible to please God our Savior without faith (Hebrews 11:6). Then in step two we talked about how serious God is about His bride the church getting sin out of their lives because He abhors sin (Leviticus 26:27-30). We also saw how persistent willful disobedience against God can cause Him to take it as a sign that that person doesn't have saving faith, but rather their faith is dead (James 2:14-26).

In the third step we talked about how not only must our bridegroom Jesus know us as His bride when He returns, but we must also know Him as our Master too. From there we learned how we cannot truly know our Master without knowing our Master's business, and how it's not possible to know our Master's business without reading the Word of God, because our Master is the Word! (John 1:14).

At the end of the third step, I mentioned that it seems like being able to do all this would be a daunting task and asked the question how was one supposed to do it. I must admit when I was writing those words, I felt concern too. It does seem like too much for someone to be able to do on their own. I can see now that step four, living our lives as a living sacrifice to God, must follow step three. Otherwise, there will be no way to faithfully continue to do everything we've talked about so far, as well as the remaining steps after that.

So now let's discuss living one's life as a sacrifice to God, and we should do that by asking a few questions. What does it mean to live one's life as a living sacrifice to God? Where do we find the motivation to live our lives as a sacrifice to God? What does it look like to live our lives as a sacrifice to God, and how do we *really* do it? That last question will make more sense after we answer the first three.

Typically, when we think of something being sacrificed, we think of it being given up; and it's no different here. However, there are levels to a sacrifice. Some things are sacrificed only for a time. Others may be sacrificed completely, even unto death if what is being sacrificed was alive; and it is this latter level of sacrifice unto death that we are talking about for ourselves.

When a person becomes a believer in Christ, God's Word says that person becomes crucified with Jesus (Romans 6:6). This is a figurative statement, of course, most believers don't actually get crucified like Jesus was, but the meaning could not be more clear. Those who have been called as believers in Christ are expected to lose their life, to sacrifice it, for God their Savior (Matthew 16:25). This is done because the person they once were without Christ is now dead (Colossians 3:3), and they have become a new person through faith in Him (2 Corinthians 5:17).

Jesus calls this being born again (John 3:6-7), and He said being born again is necessary to see the kingdom of God (John 3:3). Now this led to some confusion among the people at that time as they thought the kingdom of God on this earth was something that could be seen. However, Jesus clarified this when He said the kingdom of God is not something that can be seen right now, rather it is something that takes place inside anyone who believes in Him (Luke 17:20). This change that takes place inside a believer gives understanding to what it means to be crucified with Christ.

Chapter 4: Live Your Life as a Sacrifice to God

God's Word says believers always carry around the death of Jesus in their body, so they can also experience the life Jesus brings to them as well (2 Corinthians 4:10). It works like this, after we have been crucified with Christ through faith in Him, it is no longer we who live, but Christ who lives in us; and the life we now live is lived through faith in the One who loved us, and gave Himself up for us (Galatians 2:20). This is what it means for a believer to die to the things of this world, and to focus on God and what He wants for their life (Galatians 6:14). That is what it means to live your life as a sacrifice to God.

That's all well and good, but once we know what it means to live our lives as a living sacrifice to God, where do we as believers find the motivation needed to put it into practice. Remember, it will not be possible to do most of the steps to hearing, 'Well done, good and faithful servant,' if we do not live our lives as a sacrifice to God. The steps get progressively more challenging and we will need to live more like Christ, and less like ourselves, if we are going to be able to do them. So where do we find the motivation to do that?

My intention, at some point, was to start giving you examples from my life on how I've been trying to do many of the steps described in this book, and now seems like a good time to start doing that. Living one's life as a living sacrifice to God is not easy, especially for someone who lived the first thirty years of their life without Him like I did. While I can't imagine my life without God anymore, I lived my life as a slave to sin for thirty years before God graciously called me out of the darkness (Ephesians 5:8), and my body is just not going to give that up willingly (1 Peter 2:11).

Believers will always have their sinful flesh trying to pull them away from God (Romans 7:18-25), and it seems like for someone who lived such a long time satisfying the sinful flesh like I did, that my flesh would want to go back to that state even more than someone who grew up in the church and wasn't so 'experienced' at gratifying their sinful nature as I was. Nevertheless, whether you grew up in the church or just came to know Christ as your Savior, Bridegroom and Master while reading this book, finding motivation to live your life as a living sacrifice to God is a good thing. So let me share with you how I go about doing that.

I always find it very helpful to focus on four things about God the Father, my Savior Jesus, and the Holy Spirit as motivation to live my life as a living sacrifice to God. I try to focus on who God is, what He has done for me, the fact that God's Word is filled with commands for me to change the way I used to live my life, and to put both Him and others ahead of myself. Now each of those focus points could fill an entire book on their own, but since we don't have space for that, here are a few things to consider and I trust God will show you more as you read His Word.

God is called the Everlasting Father (Isaiah 9:6), He has always been, and He always will be (Isaiah 44:6). There has never been a time when God has not existed (Psalm 90:2), and it's the reason God told Moses His name was I Am (Exodus 3:14); because He has no beginning or end (Revelation 1:8).

God is the great Creator. He can create things and make them appear from nothing (Hebrews 11:3) by speaking them into existence (Genesis 1:3, 6, 9, 11, 14, 20, 24). His Word says He made everything in six 24-hour days (Genesis 1:31). A universe so big we still cannot measure its size, nor count its stars; but God knows how big it is (Job 9:8), and how many stars there are (Psalm 147:4). Everything in the universe is designed to bring Him glory (Psalm 19:1-2), and He sustains it all to this day (Colossians 1:17, NLT).

Whenever I stop to think about the fact that God always has been, that there has never been a time where God did not exist, that He created everything by speaking it into existence, and that He sustains it all every day, it gives me such feelings of amazement and awe that I cannot put it into words...but there is more.

God is also the King of kings (Revelation 19:16). He sets up kings and removes them (Daniel 2:21). He is always sovereign over all of them, and He directs their hearts like a river (Proverbs 21:1). If He can do that with a king, He can certainly do it in my life too (Proverbs 16:9). It is very sobering to know that what God wants to happen will happen (Isaiah 46:10); whether for a king's life, or for yours or for mine. And it is because God is able to both foresee and direct things toward future events (at the same time) that He can write the end from the beginning in His Word (same verse).

These are just a few things describing who God is and what He can do; and keeping these things at the forefront of your mind will go a long way to helping you live your life as a living sacrifice to God. However, I find even more motivation to live my life as a living sacrifice to Him by considering what God has done for me already.

God is the Author of my salvation (Hebrews 5:9). He knew what He was going to do to redeem me the day that Adam rebelled against God and sin entered the world (Genesis 3:15). He even knew what He was going to do to redeem me before He created the world (Ephesians 1:4-5). He was going to become a person in the form of Jesus Christ (John 1:10-14), live a perfect life in order to be the perfect sacrifice for my sin (Hebrews 7:25-27), die on the cross to take the punishment that I deserve (1 John 2:2, 4:10), and be raised to life again so that I can have eternal life with Him in heaven (1 Peter 1:3-4). He did all this so I will not have to spend eternity in a lake of fire (Revelation 20:15).

This is what God did for me, and for you. God bought you for a price, and you are now His in body and soul (1 Corinthians 6:20). Remember when we talked about how the Bridegroom would pay a price to the father for the bride He wanted to marry? Jesus paid a huge price to God the Father for you (Matthew 20:18-19). He did this willingly (John 10:17-18), because He knew if He did, eventually you would be born at His appointed time (Acts 17:26) and become someone who was redeemed by His blood on the cross (1 Peter 1:9). And now that Jesus has defeated death for you (2 Timothy 1:10), He has freed you from having to live your entire life fearing death (Hebrews 2:15).

Is all this not enough to live our lives as a living sacrifice to God? If He did nothing else but this, it would be enough; but there is more, much more.

Because Jesus died for you on the cross and was raised to life again for your justification (Romans 4:25), through your faith in Him –

- You are no longer considered dead by God (1 John 5:12)
- You are no longer separated from God (John 17:9-10)
- You can know the One who created you (Colossians 1:16, 21-22)

- You can live the life that God intended for you from the beginning of time (Ephesians 1:4-11)
- You can live a life filled with good works (Ephesians 2:10), and even the smallest good work done for Christ will receive a reward (Mark 9:41)
- You can live a life that's not filled with fear (2 Timothy 1:7), but one that's filled with hope (Titus 1:2)
- You can know for certain that all the promises from God about how wonderful heaven is are true (1 Corinthians 2:9)

The list could go on and on, and it's a wonderful thing that God has already done so much for us as believers in Christ, but there is another reason why we as believers can find motivation to live our lives as a sacrifice to God – He commands us to do so.

Each one of us was created by God in our mother's womb (Psalm 139:13), and because God created us, we cannot tell Him we know better than He does about how we should live our lives (Isaiah 29:16). How can someone tell God they know better than He does about anything? God's ways are not our ways, and His thoughts are not our thoughts (Isaiah 55:8-9). We simply must accept the fact that God knows better than we do regarding how we should live our lives; and His Word says we are supposed to live our lives as a sacrifice to Him (Romans 12:1).

So, what does that look like? Living our lives as a sacrifice to God? To find the answers to this question there is no better place to start than by looking in the book of Romans, chapter 12, which the apostle Paul begins by saying, *'I urge you, brothers and sisters, in view of God's mercy, to offer your bodies as a living sacrifice, holy and pleasing to God – this is your true and proper worship'* (verse 1, NIV). He then goes on to list many things believers are to do (and not do) to accomplish this –

- We are not to live in this world as nonbelievers live (verse 2)
- We are not to be puffed up with pride, rather to be humble in spirit (verse 3)
- We are to recognize that we are part of the body of Christ, that we each have a particular function within that body, and we have a

Chapter 4: Live Your Life as a Sacrifice to God

duty to perform that function, because we all belong to each other (verses 4-5)

- We are to know what our spiritual gifts are (see chapter 9), and to use them (verses 6-8)
- We are to be devoted to one another in love, hate what is evil, cling to what is good, and honor one another above ourselves (verses 9-10)
- We are never to lose our motivation to serve the Lord, rather to be joyful in hope, patient in suffering, faithful in prayer, always sharing with the Lord's people who are in need, and to practice hospitality (verses 11-13)
- We are to bless those who persecute us, not to curse them, rejoice with those who rejoice, mourn with those who mourn, live in harmony with each other, be willing to associate with people of low position, and not be conceited (verses 14-16)
- We are not to repay anyone evil for evil, to be careful to do what is right in the eyes of everyone, to live at peace with everyone, not to take revenge, but leave revenge to the Lord, and to overcome evil with good (verses 17-21)

This is a lot to consider, but there is more. Since we were raised to new life again with Christ, we are to seek heavenly things (Colossians 3:1). We are to count everything in this world as a loss compared to knowing our Lord Jesus (Philippians 3:7-8). We are to put to death within us fornication, uncleanness, lust, evil desires, greed, anger, rath, malice, blasphemy, filthy language and lying (Colossians 3:5, 8-9). Instead, we are to put on tender mercies, kindness, humility, gentleness, patience, forgiveness, love, peace and thankfulness (verses 12-15). We are also to have the Word of God in our hearts, and are told to do everything in the name of the Lord Jesus (verses 16-17).

This is only part of what God's Word says about what it looks like to live your life as a living sacrifice to God. There is much, much more that could be included. Does all this seem overwhelming? If we're honest, the answer is yes. So now we come to the final question that was asked earlier and should make much more sense now – How do we *really* do all this?

What was said earlier about finding motivation to help live our lives as a sacrifice to God is good, and it does help. However, if we were left just to ourselves to do this, it would be an impossible task. Fortunately, God hasn't left us all by ourselves.

In chapter two we talked about our dependence on God's Holy Spirit living inside us to help get sin out of our lives. How we can't do it on our own because, even though believers have been made alive in Christ (Ephesians 2:5), we also still have our sinful nature that was there from birth (Psalm 51:5); and there is nothing good about the sinful nature (Romans 7:18). So, in the same way, when we talk about living our lives as a living sacrifice to God, the only way it can be done is by submitting to God's Holy Spirit living inside us (2 Timothy 1:13-14).

Here are some things to consider.

A believer's body is a temple for God's Holy Spirit living inside them (1 Corinthians 6:19). Now stop and think about that for a minute. As a believer, you have the Lord God living inside you, right now. The One who created everything, who created you. The One who went to the cross for you is living inside you right now through the Holy Spirit (Romans 8:9, Galatians 4:6). Can you feel Him there? I hope you can. If you cannot feel Him there, don't despair. It may be easier for a more mature Christian to feel His presence inside them than for a new believer. We just need to trust Jesus when He said it was for our benefit that He was going back to heaven after He was resurrected from the dead. Because if He did not go back, God the Father would not send the Holy Spirit to the believers, both then and now (John 16:7). But Jesus did go back to heaven (Acts 1:9-11), and God the Father did send the Holy Spirit (Acts 2:1-4); and it is only because believers have the Holy Spirit living inside them that is it possible for us to want to live our lives as a sacrifice to God (Philippians 2:13).

Here are some more ways the Holy Spirit helps us. The Holy Spirit gives understanding of God's Word (Corinthians 2:14). He is what God uses to remind us of everything that God has said in His Word (John 14:17), and the Spirit living inside us can guide us into all truth (John 16:13). The Holy Spirit gives us personal discipline in our lives (2

Chapter 4: Live Your Life as a Sacrifice to God

Timothy 1:7), He allows us to resist the devil (James 4:7), and He makes us strong in our weaknesses (2 Corinthians 12:9). He searches our hearts to find and remove sinful things (Psalm 139:22-23), and He changes us to be more like Christ (1 Corinthians 3:17-18).

That is how we really live our lives as a living sacrifice to God, by submitting to the Holy Spirit and allowing Him do it for us. It's not complicated, but submitting to the Holy Spirit means we also must make changes in how we treat our physical bodies.

Our body is a temple of the Holy Spirit and it belongs to God (1 Corinthians 6:19), so we must take care of it. This means things like avoiding sexual immorality at all costs (verse 18), because sexual immorality also affects God's Holy Spirit inside us (verses 15-17). It means we must give our body the proper nourishment it needs and protect it from injury (Ephesians 5:29). It means understanding that not only do our bodies belong to God, but they also belong to others as well.

If you are married, the man's body is not only his, but also his wife's, and the wife's body is not only hers, but also her husband's (1 Corinthians 7:4). In the same way, all believers are part of each other in that we are all part of the body of Christ (12:12-14). This means not taking care of your body will have a negative impact on the health of the body of Christ as a whole (verses 21-25). Remember, we all have a function we are supposed to play in the body of Christ (verses 17-19), and if one believer suffers from neglecting their own body, the entire body of Christ suffers too (verse 26).

There are many reasons why we must take care in how we use our physical bodies while on this earth, not the least of which is because God's Word says a believer who does not possess their own body in a way that is holy and honorable rejects God who gave them the Holy Spirit! Did you know that? (Thessalonians 4:3-8)

So, as believers, let us take care of our physical bodies, as well as our spiritual bodies (1 Corinthians 15:44-46), and in doing so we will truly be living every aspect of our lives as a living sacrifice to God; and be one step closer to hearing, 'Well done, good and faithful servant,' when we come face to face with Jesus for the first time.

Well Done, Good and Faithful Servant

Chapter 5

Make Prayer a Priority in Your Life

Conversation is the foundation of any meaningful relationship between two people. It is no different with us and God, and prayer is that method of conversation that we use to communicate with Him. I was surprised (and I wasn't) to hear that so few Christians devote any significant amount of time to prayer in their daily lives.(1)

How can you have a relationship with someone if you don't talk to them? How can you be engaged to be married to someone and not talk to them? How many friends do you have that you do not talk to? How many teachers have you had where there was no communication between you and them? The examples can go on and on, but it should be obvious that spending time in prayer with God should be a big part of any believer's life.

Now I said that I was, and I wasn't, surprised to hear that so few Christians spend a significant amount of time in prayer every day. I was surprised because it seems so obvious how important it is. But I also wasn't surprised because, honestly, the necessity of spending sufficient time in prayer with God escaped my attention for many years after I became a Christian. I remember the day clearly when God showed me that I needed to be spending a lot more time in prayer than I was.

I had been on my church council for a couple of years and was even serving as treasurer for the church. This was no small task because the church operates a pre-K through eighth grade school as well. The finances for both the church and the school were quite extensive and required me to get some help from an accountant at first; but needless to say, I felt pretty good about what I was doing to serve God in this way. However, the third year on the council God brought a woman of prayer to serve with us. She accepted the position without really thinking she had anything to offer the group, but decided she would be obedient to His calling and join the council anyway. Little did I know how much of an impact she was going to have on my life.

She came to the first monthly meeting and we spent our two hours as usual going over the finances of the church and the school, talking about any pressing issues and everything seemed to me to go well. This continued for another month or two until she had the boldness and wisdom to speak up about how she now understood why God wanted her to be on the council. She said she was surprised that for something as significant as a council charged with setting policies for running a church and school that we spent so little time in prayer during the meetings. We would open the meeting with a quick prayer and close it the same way, but spent no significant time talking to the very One whose input was needed to make sure everything was being done according to His will.

There was a profound silence in the room, at least that's the way I recall it, and I was cut to the heart that she was correct. Not only that, but I realized right away that even though I was trying to live my life genuinely wanting to do God's will, I wasn't spending nearly enough time in prayer as I should every day to help make that happen. From that point on, the council made an immediate adjustment to how we spent those two hours. We took 20-30 minutes each meeting to go around the table and present our prayers to God; and I made an immediate adjustment to my own prayer life as well trying to spend at least 30 minutes in prayer on bended knee every day.

I am embarrassed to admit that I've spent more than half the time I've been a Christian without understanding the importance of prayer, and I'm sure it stunted the growth of my faith for years. However, as God promises to make all things turn out for good for those who love Him and are called according to His purpose (Romans 8:28), the good that has come out of that is it has made me feel like I have to make up for lost time and now prayer is a much bigger part of my life. It also benefits anyone reading this book too because not only does it make sure prayer is included as one of the steps to hearing, 'Well done good and faithful servant,' but it's given me a desire to learn much more about what God's Word says about prayer and pass it on to you.

Chapter 5: Make Prayer a Priority in Your Life

So what does the Bible say about prayer? A lot. There's way more than can be covered in one chapter of a book; indeed there are whole books on the subject of prayer. However, that doesn't mean we can't learn a bit more and improve our prayer life with God no matter where we currently are. To do this, I think it would be best to take much of what God's Word says about prayer and divide it into four categories. What we can do to make sure our prayers are heard, how we are to pray, what we are to pray for, and examples of prayers that caused God to act.

What can we do to make our prayers heard? This must undoubtedly be at the top of the list as we can go on praying all we want to God, but it won't do any good if He chooses not to hear us. That may come as a surprise to a lot of people, but the Bible says there are many things that can hinder our prayers from reaching God. Now let me clarify something first. God knows every word we speak, even before the word is done being spoken (Psalm 139:4). That's amazing! And even believers will have to stand (same as unbelievers) and attest for every careless word that we said (Matthew 12:36, NIV). So God knows every word we speak, whether they are directed to Him in prayer or not. The difference is, we can hinder the ability of our prayers to be heard by God by doing a lot of things wrong.

The importance of knowing this cannot be understated. In fact, this is the one area from God's Word on prayer that I'm going to include everything I've learned and was able to find in searching the Bible to prepare for writing this chapter. I'm not going to go into a lot of specifics on most of them, as they are pretty self-explanatory. Rather I will trust that the Holy Spirit will give you understanding and/or conviction if any of these are areas in your life that need improvement in order to make your prayers more readily heard by God. There are two I'm going to start with and then will provide you a list of the others.

The first thing that must happen for your prayers to be heard by God is you must be praying to Him, the One True God as revealed in His Word. God says He is the only God who ever existed, and there is no God but Him (Isaiah 44:6). If you don't believe this, you are praying to a God that doesn't exist. God's Word says He is triune in nature. He exists in three persons, God the Father, God the Son Jesus, and God the Holy Spirit

(Matthew 28:19). Three persons yet all the same God (1 John 5:7). If you don't believe this you are praying to a God that doesn't exist. God says He sent His one and only Son to be a perfect sacrifice for your sins, so that you may believe on His Son Jesus and have everlasting life (John 3:16). If you don't believe this, you are praying to a God that doesn't exist, and should not be surprised that your prayers are not being heard.

The second thing that must happen for your prayers to be heard by God is you must be obedient to His commands. Prayers from people who are disobedient to God's commands, whether believers or not, are an abomination to Him (Proverbs 28:9). This actually encompasses many of the ways that we can hinder our prayers to God, through our disobedience. We must be obedient to Him if we want our prayers to be heard, and possibly answered.

We also need to pay special attention to these areas as well –

- We must humble ourselves and repent before God for Him to hear (2 Chronicles 7:14)

- We must confess our sin or God will not hear (Psalm 66:18)

- Praying with humility makes our prayers heard by God (Daniel 10:12)

- Those who pray with godly fear will be heard (Hebrews 5:7)

- We must pray in faith that God can answer our prayers (James 1:6-7)

- Treating a spouse poorly will hinder our prayers (1 Peter 3:7)

- God ears are open to those who obey Him, but not to those who practice evil (verse 12)

- Praying for anything that is according to the will of God will be heard (1 John 5:14)

So now that we have a better understanding of things to do and not do so that we can be sure God will hear our prayers, what does God's Word say about how we should pray? I should clarify that by 'how' I mean how often should we pray and where should we pray. After we establish the

Chapter 5: Make Prayer a Priority in Your Life

answers to those questions, then we will talk about what the content of our prayers should be.

The Bible tells us to pray without ceasing (1 Thessalonians 5:17) and to bring everything to God in prayer (Philippians 4:6). Now this may at first seem overwhelming. How are we to do anything else if every minute of every day we are to be praying? Well, hold on a minute. The Bible also says we should not pray in public to garner the praise of people but rather we should pray in private (Matthew 6:5-6). However, we can't stay locked up in a room in prayer our whole life either so what is God's Word really saying here?

I think the best way to answer that question is to look at God's own prayer life when He was living on earth in the person of Jesus. Whatever we record Jesus doing in regards to prayer is something we can be sure would please God if we were to imitate Him as our pattern for prayer. Now I'm certainly aware it won't be possible for us to have the exact same prayer life Jesus did because Jesus is God and God would of course have the perfect prayer life; as sinful human beings we simply cannot. However, by looking at what we see in the Bible about Jesus' prayer life and trying our best to imitate Him, we can be sure that kind of prayer life will be pleasing to God.

The first thing we observe is Jesus prayed a lot, and He was very intentional about setting aside time to be in prayer alone with God the Father. We are told Jesus would get up early in the morning and go to a solitary place to pray (Mark 1:35). He did this because He knew that when the others in His 'family' got up they would be demanding His attention (verse 36). Even when His fame spread and He would spend all day teaching and healing others, He would still find time to go to a secluded place to be in prayer (Luke 5:16). This means if we are going to try to pray the way Jesus did, we have to find time every day to be alone with God in prayer. It's that important.

We read in one place in the Bible that Jesus stayed up in prayer all night (Luke 6:12), and my guess would be this was not just a single occasion. We are told that Jesus did so many things during His three years of ministry that if they were all written down the whole world could not contain the books that would be required (John 21:25). As Jesus spent more and more of His days teaching and healing the people, there was probably little time to do anything else, so He most likely would have spent more than just one whole night in prayer.

The point I'm trying to make here is that prayer time was more important to Jesus than sleep. If it was that important for Him, it should be very important for us to find time to be in prayer alone with God every day. Whether you choose to sleep less and get up early to pray or stay up late to find time for prayer, or whether you choose to be more intentional throughout your day to find times to pray, the goal should be spending more than just a couple minutes in prayer each day and thinking that will be pleasing to God; because it won't.

Jesus also prayed in the Spirit, meaning He prayed through the power of the Holy Spirit (Luke 10:21), and this is something we are told we should do as well (Ephesians 6:18). I believe praying through (and to) the Holy Spirit living inside us is what allows us to pray without ceasing and to be constantly in prayer. God's Word says the Holy Spirit that is inside the hearts of believers prays on their behalf (Romans 8:26), so even if we are not constantly praying in our minds or talking out loud to God, the Spirit is praying for us too.

This also allows us to be able to do another of the suggestions for prayer found in His Word where we are told to pray everywhere (1 Timothy 2:8). Remember how we said we were going to try to answer the question of how do we spend a significant portion of our day in prayer without being by ourselves in a room, or avoiding public prayer that seeks glory from people instead of glory from God? (Matthew 6:5). We could already look at the life of Jesus and know He didn't do that, but we can be sure this is how we can fulfill God's commands to pray without ceasing and to pray everywhere; by constantly praying in the Spirit (Hebrews 13:15).

So now that we have a better idea of how often we should pray (a lot) and where (everywhere), what should the content of our prayers be? Well, to answer this we should also look to God's own prayer life in Jesus because we can be sure if we follow the pattern that Jesus used, it will be pleasing to God.

Chapter 5: Make Prayer a Priority in Your Life

Jesus was very intentional regarding the content of His prayers and He gave us what is known as the model prayer in Matthew chapter 6. Jesus said our prayers should include praise to God (verse 9), the desire to see His will be done in the world and in our own lives (verse 10), the understanding that God sustains us (verse 11), confession and repentance for our sins (verse 12), calling on His protection (verse 13), and finishing with more praise (ibid). These were given not only as a model for the content of our prayers, but also in an order in which we should pray.

We see Jesus also using this model in the longest recorded prayer in the Bible in John, chapter 17. Of course, He had no need to confess any sin, as He lived a sinless life (John 8:46, Hebrews 4:15), but all the other steps are there along with another one that we should use as well. Jesus began by praising God the Father and giving Him glory for the ministry that was done while He (Jesus) was on the earth (verses 1-3). He then asked the Father to see His will be done in Jesus' soon to be sacrifice on the cross (verses 4-5). Next Jesus prayed for His disciples, that the Father would sustain them after He was gone (verses 6-13), and that He would protect them from Satan and the world that hates them (verses 14-19). Jesus then prays for all believers for all time, which includes you and me, that we would all be one in Christ Jesus (verses 20-22), and that the world will be receptive to our witness of the gospel through a kind of love evident in our lives that can only come from God (verse23). Jesus then finishes His prayer with some very high praise to God the Father (verses 24-26).

There was an additional step there that we are also commanded to practice, praying for others (1 Timothy 2:1), and it should be noted that it pleases God when we pray for other people, particularly for their salvation (verses 2-3). However, we should recognize its proper place when we are praying an extended prayer to God; only after we have praised Him for who He is, what He has done for us, and what He will continue to do for us in and through Christ Jesus. So, Jesus' prayer in John 17, and the examples we already saw from Paul's letters, show us there are other things we can, and should, include in our prayers to God.

Here are some more things we should pray for (and one we should not) when praying to God –

- We should pray that we will escape the coming wrath of God and stand before Jesus our Redeemer in salvation (Luke 21:36)
- We should pray for justice (Luke 18:1-7)
- We should pray for others who are struggling (Romans 15:30)
- We should pray that we fulfill God's will for our lives (1 Thessalonians 1:11)
- We should pray in thanksgiving for the food God has given us, including the flesh of animals that God gave us to eat (1 Timothy 4:3-5)
- We should pray with tears and loud cries if moved to do so (Hebrews 5:7)
- We should not ask for more to spend on ourselves (James 4:3)
- We should pray for those who are sick (James 5:14-15)
- We should pray for ourselves and other believers to live a more holy life (James 5:16)
- We should cast all our cares on Him in prayer (1 Peter 5:7)

Now all of these things are good to pray for, and we should pray for all of them, but let me close this chapter by giving you some examples where prayers caused God to act. I think sometimes we can get lost in thinking that since God is sovereign, and He will ultimately do whatever He wants, that our prayers don't carry much weight with Him. So why devote so much time and attention to prayer? Well, God delights in our prayers (Proverbs 15:8), and the prayers of believers are powerful and effective with God (James 5:16b, NIV).

Here are some examples of prayer that caused God to act –

- When God sent the plagues on Egypt to get Pharoah to release His people from slavery, Moses prayed several times to God to stop the plagues and they were stopped (Exodus 8:12-13, 8:29, 9:33, 10:17-19)

Chapter 5: Make Prayer a Priority in Your Life

- When Israel created a golden calf to worship, and God told Moses He was going to destroy them because of what they had done, Moses prayed to God that He would relent and not destroy them, and God spared them (Exodus 32:10-14)
- When Gideon prayed for a sign from God as an indication that God would deliver the Midianites over to him in battle, God answered his prayer two times (Judges 6:36-40)
- When Samson prayed that God would give him his strength back one last time to push down two pillars, God did so (Judges 16:28)
- When Hannah prayed to the Lord asking for a son, God granted her request and she became the mother of Samuel the prophet (1 Samuel 1:11-12, 20)
- When king David prayed to the Lord that He would remove the plague from the land, because David had taken a census of the fighting men of Israel, God ended the plague (2 Samuel 24:25)
- When Solomon prayed before the newly built temple, he asked God to place His name and dwell there, and God responded that He would do so (1 Kings 8:22-9:3)
- When Elijah prayed to the Lord that He would return the soul of the only son of a widow that had died, God did so and the boy came alive again (1 Kings 17:21-22)
- When Elisha prayed to the Lord that He would reveal to his servant the heavenly chariots of fire that were there to fight the Syrians, God did so (2 Kings 6:17)
- When king Hezekiah fell ill and was going to die, he prayed to the Lord, and God healed him and added fifteen years to his life (2 Kings 20:2-6)
- When Nehemiah prayed to God that he would be allowed to return to Jerusalem and rebuild the city's walls, God moved king Artaxerxes to let him go (Nehemiah 2:1-6)

- When king Hezekiah prayed for deliverance from the Assyrian army that surrounded Jerusalem, the Lord killed 185,000 of them in one night, saving the city (Isaiah 38:21-22, 36)
- When Daniel prayed that Israel would be restored according to prophecy seventy years after Jerusalem fell to the Babylonians, the Lord sent the angel Gabriel to show him what would happen over the next 483 years until the Messiah Jesus would come (Daniel 9:20-27)
- When Jonah prayed to the Lord from inside the belly of the great fish (Jonah 2:1), and from Sheol after he died inside the fish (2:6), God heard and caused the fish to vomit his body onto dry ground (2:10), and God revived Jonah (3:2)
- When Zacharias prayed for a child, God heard his prayer and sent the angel Gabriel to tell him he would have a son who would be John the Baptist (Luke 1:13-17)
- When Saul (soon to be the apostle Paul) was blinded by seeing the resurrected Jesus (Acts 22:11), he prayed and God sent Ananias to restore Saul's sight (Acts 9:10-11)
- When the apostle Peter prayed to God to restore life to the body of Tabitha, who had been dead for some time (Acts 9:37-39), God did so (verse 40)
- When the apostle Peter was arrested and put in prison, the church prayed and God sent an angel to free him (Acts 12:5-10)
- Elijah prayed that it would not rain for three and a half years and God held the rain from falling until Elijah prayed that it would rain again and then God sent rain (James 5:17-18)

I probably didn't have to give you all these examples from God's Word before you could see that God answers prayer, but these were just a few examples. There are many more. Again, the point of sharing so many places in the Bible where God answered prayer is to show that the God who made everything in the universe six thousand years ago*, and sustains it all to this day, listens when we talk to Him, and will act on our

Chapter 5: Make Prayer a Priority in Your Life

prayers if He chooses to do so. This should never fail to amaze us that we have that kind of 'pull' with our Creator. King David said as much where he said when he considers everything that God has done, who is he that God should care about him (Psalm 8:3-4, NASB).

Considering everything we've learned in this chapter about prayer, what a wonderful gift it is from God if done properly, and how it is not possible to hear, 'Well done, good and faithful servant" without it,' don't you think it is foolish not to give more attention to prayer in your life?

Well Done, Good and Faithful Servant

Chapter 6

Love One Another

It was my original intention that the title of this chapter (or more accurately this step) should be a person must love one another as Jesus has loved them. However, I honestly don't think it's possible for us, in our current sinful condition, to be able to love one another as God loves us, so I kept it at one must love one another. I also stopped short of using Jesus as our measuring point because I didn't want anyone to get discouraged thinking that they couldn't do this step if the only way to do it right was to love others as Jesus loves them.

Certainly, when we consider what God's Word says about the love of Christ being beyond our knowledge (Ephesians 3:19), we cannot possibly expect to be able love others the same way Christ loved us; because an understanding of Christ's love is not attainable for us. So then how can we love others as He loves us if we can't even understand how much He loves us?

Well, while I don't think it's possible for us to love one another the same as Jesus loves us, it is certainly possible to love others *like* Jesus does. It's a subtle difference, but different enough for us to make it an attainable goal. If we treat others the same way as we would want them to treat us (Luke 6:31), there is no room for interpretation. We want to be treated exactly the same way, and I don't believe we can treat others exactly the same way Jesus did (and does), because God is going to do that perfectly. But if we treat others *like* we want to be treated, there is room for a similarity of behaviors without necessarily having them be exactly the same. Does that make sense?

So then the question may become - Why isn't the title of this step a person must love one another *like* Jesus has loved them? It is splitting hairs, I know. However, since God's Word says we can fulfill the entire law of God if we were to love our neighbors as ourselves (Galatians 5:14), yet it only mentions one person other than Jesus that was ever able to love another person like that (1 Samuel 18:13), it seems better just to say something we most certainly can do – we must love one another.

It is here though, that we must pause and make sure we understand the meaning of the word 'love' as it appears in the Bible because there are differences that need to be pointed out. God's Word was written in Hebrew (Old Testament) and Greek (New Testament), and both of those languages have more than one word that are translated as 'love,' but they mean different things. This is important to understand because God's Word makes it clear that we can and should show love to everyone (Romans 13:8-10), including those whom we don't like, and even someone we may hate (Matthew 5:44).

How are we supposed to love to someone we hate? It seems impossible, but it can be done. Actually, it can be done rather easily. This is because when we correctly translate the different Greek words for love, we see that loving someone we don't like (and even hate) doesn't necessarily have to include the *feelings* of love that a person would otherwise believe have to be there for someone speaking, say, the English language. In fact, in the majority of places in God's Word we see both the Hebrew and Greek words used for love are talking about loving more as an act of the will, and not so much loving from an emotional standpoint.

Now, I know once someone starts talking about Bible translations people can tune out, so I won't go into too much detail. However, a brief description of each word is necessary to get a better idea of how many different words are used in the Bible that translate as 'love,' and what each word means. This list will also serve another purpose. It will allow us to use the original language to give us a greater understanding of Scripture when verses are cited or referenced that contain a word translated as love, loving or loved.

Here are the root words for love in the Hebrew language and their meaning –

- Ahab (aw-hab) is the closest Hebrew word to the English equivalent of the word love in that it signifies a strong emotional attachment to another person, object or action.

Chapter 6: Love One Another

- Ahabah (a-hab-aw) is used to describe the love between a husband and wife or between friends. It is also used in the Old Testament to describe God's love for Israel.

- Dod (dode) is used to describe loving another person through action. It literally means to boil but is referring to the thoughtful action to 'boil in love' towards another person.

- Chashaq (khaw-shak) means to cling to another person in love.

Here are the main root words for love in the Greek language and their meaning –

- Agapao (ag-ap-ah'-o) refers to loving someone in both a social and moral sense and its primary use is as a verb, so the word indicates a deliberate attitude of the mind (a choice) to show love to another person through action; whether the feelings of love accompany those actions or not.

- Agape (ag-ah'-pay) is the highest form of love. It is an unconditional and sacrificial love, putting the needs of others above oneself, and is often translated 'charity' in several versions of the Bible.

- Phileo (fil-eh'-o) has an emotional meaning when referring to love and is only used 25 times in the New Testament. It is interesting to point out that God never commands us to love Him using this word, agapao or agape is always used instead. There are places where phileo is used to describe God's love towards Jesus, and us, but we are never commanded to love Him back in that way. Probably because this would conflict with the commandment that we are to fear God too.

Now I wanted to include the words for love from both the *Old* and New Testaments because I have seen many word studies, and heard many pastors talk about the different Greek words translated as 'love,' but I haven't seen any about the kind and amount of Hebrew words for love; which are found at least 340 times in the Old Testament (depending on the version of the Bible). Many of those words are used to describe God's love for people, His desire to be loved in return, and how the relationship between a person and God was to be done in and through love; even before Jesus came.

It's a shame most people aren't aware of the number of times the words love, loving or loved are used in the Old Testament, which is probably why it has a bad reputation of only depicting God as being One who is vengeful and full of wrath. Rather than a loving God who takes no pleasure when someone dies and goes to hell, but wants people to turn to Him and be saved (Ezekiel 33:11). God does not change (Malachi 3:6), so the God we see in the New Testament is the same God from the Old Testament; a God of love, a God who *is* love (1 John 4:7-8).

This is the main reason why we must love one another, because God is love. But it goes even farther than that. God's Word says if we don't show love to one another, especially other Christians (1 John 3:14), then it is an indication that we do not know God (1 John 4:8). And if we do not know God, then we are not saved (John 17:3). Are you starting to see why it is so important that as believers we love one another? It will be impossible to hear, 'Well done good and faithful servant,' if we are not saved, but it will also be impossible to hear those words if we do not love one another, because God is love.

So what did Jesus, who is God (Romans 9:5), say about love? If we are being transformed into the likeness of Jesus, then we should look at what He said regarding love, and how we are to love God and others. I think the best way to do this would be to list many of the verses from God's Word that were said by Jesus about love. And when you see the Greek word that is used for 'love,' it will give you a much better idea of what Jesus (God) meant by the commandment or statement regarding love. This will be a long list but well worth the study; because if we are going to love God and one another the way He wants us to, we need to have a better understanding of what God is saying when He talks about love.

- *"You have heard it said, 'You shall agapao your neighbor and hate your enemy.' But I say to you, agapao your enemies, bless those who curse you, do good to those who hate you, and pray for those who spitefully use you and persecute you...for if you agapao*

Chapter 6: Love One Another

(only) those who love you, what reward have you?" – Matthew 5:43-44, 46 (word added for clarification)

- *"Honor your father and your mother, and you shall agapao your neighbor as yourself."* – Matthew 19:19

- *"And because lawless will abound (in the last days), the agape of many will grow cold."* – Matthew 24:12 (words added for clarification)

- *"And you shall agapao the Lord your God with all your heart, with all your soul, with all your mind, and with all your strength.' This is the first commandment. And the second, like it, is this: 'You shall agapao your neighbor as yourself.' There is no commandment greater than these."* – Mark 12:30-31

- *"And to agapao Him with all the heart, with all the understanding, with all the soul, and with all the strength, and to agapao one's neighbor as oneself, is more than all the whole burnt offerings and sacrifices."* – Mark 12:33

- *"But agapao your enemies, do good, and lend, hoping for nothing in return; and your reward will be great, and you will be sons of the Most High. For He is kind to the unthankful and evil."* – Luke 6:35

- *"But woe to you Pharisees! For you tithe mint and rue and all manner of herbs, and pass by the justice and agape of God. These you ought to have done (tithing), without leaving the others undone."* – Luke 11:42 (word added for clarification)

- *"But I know you (Jewish leaders), that you do not have the agape of God in you."* – John 5:42 (words added for clarification)

- *"Jesus said to them (Jewish leaders), "If God were your Father, you would agapao Me, for I proceeded forth and came from God; nor have I come of Myself, but He sent Me."* – John 8:42 (words added for clarification)

- "He who phileo his life will lose it, and he who hates his life in this world will keep it for eternal life." – John 12:25
- "A new commandment I give to you, that you agapao one another; so as I have agapao you, so you must agapao one another." – John 13:34
- "If you agapao me, keep My commandments." – John 14:15
- Jesus answered him (His disciple Jude), "If anyone agapao Me, he will keep My word; and My Father will agapao him, and We will come and make Our home with him. He who does not agapao Me, does not keep My words." – John 14:23-24a (words added for clarification)
- "As the Father has agapao Me, I also have agapao you; abide in My agape. If you keep My commandments, you will abide in My agape, just as I have kept My Father's commandments and abide in His agape...This is My commandment, that you apapao one another as I have agapao you." – John 15:9-10, 12
- "Greater agape has no one than this, than to lay down one's life for his friends." – John 15:13
- "For the Father Himself phileo you, because you have phileo Me, and have believed that I came forth from God." – John 16:27
- "And I have declared to them Your name (Father), and will declare it, that the agape with which You agapao Me may be in them, and I in them." – John 17:26 (word added for clarification)
- "Jesus said to Simon Peter, "Simon, son of Jonah, do you agapao Me more than these?" He said to Him, "Yes, Lord; You know that I phileo You." – John 21:15
- "Jesus said to him a second time, "Simon, son of Jonah, do you agapao Me?" He said to Him, "Yes, Lord; You know that I phileo You." – John 21:16
- "He said to him the third time, "Simon, son of Jonah, do you phileo Me?" Peter was grieved because He said to him the third

time, "Do you love Me?" And he said to Him, "Lord, you know all things; You know that I phileo You." – John 21:17

These are many of the words we see in the four Gospels where Jesus talks about love. In addition to showing how Jesus commands us to love one another, I also included a few verses where Jesus was also talking about the love that He and God the Father have for each other, and for us, because this is helpful in our overall understanding why we are supposed to love one another.

Ultimately, it's because the love that believers have inside them comes from God (1 John 4:7), and when God sends His Holy Spirit to live inside a believer, the Spirit not only brings the agape of God into that person (Romans 5:5), but He also empowers them to show that agape love back to the Father, Jesus and everyone else (I John 4:16).

Hopefully you can now see that agapao means showing love to another person through action, while agape is used more as a noun in referring to the overall love of God. We also see that God loves us using the emotional based word for love – phileo – and that we can (as Peter did) love God back in that way too. However, I would like to point something out in these verses that may not be apparent at first glance.

I mentioned before that God never commands us to phileo Him purely from an emotional standpoint, and that is true. There is no commandment to love God in the original Greek translations using the word phileo. However, that means that every time we are commanded in the New Testament to love God, by use of the word agapao, this implies it is ultimately a decision that we must make to either do it, or not do it; because the word itself describes a conscious attitude of the mind to show love to someone – it's a choice.

Jesus knows this, which is why He commanded us to abide (to remain) in the love of God.

"As the Father has agapao Me, I also have agapao you; abide in My agape. If you keep My commandments, you will abide in My agape, just as I have kept My Father's commandments and abide in His agape." – John 15:9-10

Why would Jesus command us to remain in the agape of God if it was not a choice for us to do so? It is a choice. So then, if it is a choice for us to love God or not to love Him, shouldn't this step be called - One must love God, and one another? It could have been, but it seems to me there was a problem in the early church where believers were showing much love to God but not so much love to each other. This made the apostles want to put a stronger emphasis in their letters on loving one another; even above loving God. Unfortunately, despite their best efforts to correct this problem, it continues even to this day.

There are currently way too many Christians who show love to God by going to church, reading His Word and through prayer, but don't show much love to others. It's good that they are trying to love God, but what kind of love are they really showing Him if they don't love His children? If someone says they love me, yet doesn't want anything to do with my own children, that would cause me to doubt the sincerity of their love. We are told love must be sincere (Romans 12:9), so if we are going to show sincere love to God, we must also love His children, our brothers and sisters in Christ.

The early apostles knew this which is why we see such things in their letters as *above all things* we should put on love (Colossians 3:14) and *above all* we should have fervent unfailing love for one another (1 Peter 4:8). Therefore, since God's Word says it *is* possible to fulfill every commandment in the law by loving one another (including the commandment to love God), and since the apostles spent so much time in their letters telling us to love one another, and since most Christians have more trouble loving other people than God, let's keep the focus where it should be - on loving one another.

So what does that look like - loving one another - and how do we do it? Thankfully, God's Word doesn't just tell us to love one another and not show us what that's like.

When we are truly loving one another –

- We show mercy to one another (Luke 6:36)
- We honor one another above ourselves (Romans 12:10)
- We do good to everyone (Romans 12:17)

- We live at peace with everyone (Romans 12:18)
- We share the gospel with others, that Christ died for the forgiveness of their sins (1 Corinthians 5:14-20)
- We are patient and kind with one another, not envious or boastful (1 Corinthians 13:4, NIV)
- We are not easily angered by others, and keep no record of how many times someone hurts us (verse 5, NIV)
- We protect one another, trust one another, and persevere with one another (verse 6, NIV)
- We bear with one another (2 Corinthians 4:2)
- We speak the truth to one another (2 Corinthians 4:15)
- We comfort one another (Philippians 2:1)
- We don't do things out of selfish ambition, but put the needs of others first (Philippians 2:3)
- We share what we have with one another (Hebrews 13:16)
- When we see another believer in need, we do something about it (1 John 3:17)

This is not all that God's Word says about what it looks like to love one another, but it's a good start; and I would encourage you to read these sections of the Bible, and others, to learn more.

So now that we have a better idea of what it looks like to love one another, how do we *really* do it? Thankfully, God's Word is not silent about that either. The Bible says we love because God first loved us (1 John 4:19), and our ability to love in these ways, and others, is only made possible because the love of God has been poured into our hearts by the Holy Spirit living inside us (Romans 5:5). We read also in God's Word that we were given a Spirit of love (2 Timothy 1:7), that we are taught by God (through the Spirit) to love one another (2 Thessalonians 4:9-10), and that the first 'fruit' of the Spirit is love (Galatians 5:22). So, by all this we can be sure that it is only through God's Holy Spirit that we are able to do these things.

It is good that God designed it this way, that we have to rely on the Holy Spirit inside us to do something that is so important to hearing, "Well done, good and faithful servant," because if it were left to ourselves to love one another, we would fail.

Before we move on to the next step, I would like to leave you with a few more thoughts that are important to consider.

Love is greater than the faith that saves us (1 Corinthians 13:3). Did you know that? Most believers are familiar with 1 Corinthians 13, and I did list some of the things the apostle Paul said that love is in order to show us ways that we can love other people. However, even though I've read verse 13:3 dozens of times, it took a while before it occurred to me that when Paul speaks of faith, hope and love, and that the greatest of them is love, that he is actually saying love is greater than the faith that saves us. Once I realized that, it really made me understand how important it is that we love one another (and hopefully for you too), because God choose to elevate love above the faith that saves us.

It's not surprising when you really think about it. Which of those three will be left after God makes everything new and His dwelling place with be with people again? (Revelation 21:3-4). Will faith have to exist when we will be able to see God up close? Will hope have to exist when God's promises to redeem us for all eternity have been realized? (Romans 8:24). No, only love will remain. So, now that we understand why it is so important to God that we love one another, it makes sense when we read things in His Word like if we have a faith that can literally move mountains, but have not love, we are nothing (1 Corinthians 13:2). And it also makes sense that we shouldn't expect to hear, "Well done, good and faithful servant," when we meet Jesus for the first time, if we do not love one another.

Chapter 7

Do Good Works

This step is very important and you will see why as you read through the chapter. In the same way that it will be absolutely impossible to hear "Well done, good and faithful servant," when you meet Jesus for the first time if you are not a true believer, it will also be impossible to hear those words if you don't do good works. The authors of the New Testament would not have spent so much time talking about the importance of good works for those who follow Christ if it wasn't such a big deal with God. His Word says we were redeemed in Christ Jesus for good works (Ephesians 2:10), so it's a *very* big deal with God. However, it is also important that those good works be done in the right way – out of love for God and for others, and not as a way to try to earn one's salvation; because the two verses before Ephesians 2:10 say we cannot earn our salvation through good works.

There has been great confusion for many centuries over good works and how they relate to a person's eternal salvation. There are religions that say a person cannot be saved without that person contributing good works to grace (for example Mormonism and Catholicism*), and there are religions whose entire theology is centered around having to do good works for salvation (for example, Islam and Jehovah's Witness*). However, any religion that says good works are a necessary contribution to one's salvation, or are themselves the basis for determining one's salvation, are incorrect because God's Word says in Ephesian 2:8-9 (and many other places) that it is only through faith that a person is saved; through faith in Jesus Christ (Matthew 1:21, John 14:6, Acts 4:12, Romans 10:9, 1 Timothy 1:15, Hebrews 7:25).

So if we are only saved by God's grace through faith in Christ, why is there such an emphasis on doing good works in the Bible? The answer to that question can be found in what God's Word says about the relationship between good works and saving faith – good works are an *indicator* that a person has saving faith in Christ Jesus (James 2:18), and *not* the method God uses as a means for salvation. We must understand this relationship before we continue. Why it is so critically important for a believer in Christ, who has the Holy Spirit living inside them, to do good works even though it is not the good works that contribute in any way to that person's salvation? We touched on this briefly in the first step that talked about how we first have to be a true believer in Christ and how one of the ways we can be sure we are a true believer is if we are doing good works.

There is no section of Scripture that explains this better than the book of James, chapter two. James was the half-brother of Jesus, and he did not believe Jesus was the Messiah (John 7:5) until after He was resurrected from the dead and showed Himself to James (1 Corinthians 15:7). James then went on to be the leader of the church in Jerusalem (Acts 21:17-18) and was the author of this book in the Bible. James understood the relationship of good works to saving faith and explains it in chapter two.

He said a person that claims to have faith but doesn't do good works is not saved (2:14), because faith without good works is a dead faith, and a dead faith cannot save anyone (verse 17). (We will see how Jesus confirms this is true at the end of this chapter.) James explained that we *show* we have saving faith in Christ by our good works (verse 18), then gave an example of how Abraham proved he had saving faith by offering to sacrifice his son Isaac because God told him to do so (verse 21). God did not make Abraham go through with sacrificing his son (Genesis 22:12), but the fact that he was being obedient in doing this 'good work' that God told him to do proved he had saving faith (James 2:22-24). James then says again, in case his readers missed it the first time, someone who claims to have faith in Christ that isn't doing good works has a dead faith which cannot save them (verse 24).

Now, there are a couple things that need to be pointed out here. First, I hope you can see the relationship between good works and saving faith. It is not any good work in and of itself that makes us righteous (saved); Abraham didn't even do that 'good work.' Rather, God counted Abraham

Chapter 7: Do Good Works

as righteous because he was being obedient in the 'good work' that God told him to do; and it confirmed his faith in God was real. God was testing Abraham (Genesis 22:1-2) and he passed the test proving his faith was genuine (Genesis 22:16-17).

The second thing that needs to be pointed out is this testing of Abraham has implications for us too. God says He will test us (1 Thessalonians 2:4, 1 Peter 1:7) like he tested Abraham (Hebrews 11:17) to make sure our faith is genuine. This testing will not be in the same way of sacrificing one of our children; God detests anyone who really does sacrifice children (Ezekiel 16:20-22). Rather, His Word just says He is going to test us to make sure our faith is genuine, and we can be sure the test will involve some kind of doing of good works.

The Bible says we should even test ourselves in this regard (2 Corinthians 13:5). Did you know that? The apostle Paul told the believers at Corinth to test themselves to see if they were 'in the faith' (saved) and what he meant by that was they should examine their lives to see if there was evidence of good works that show they pass the test. Paul confirmed this by saying the evidence the believers at Corinth were searching for to prove that he was an apostle (because they had been told otherwise) was found in his good works (verse 6).

The importance of good works in a believer's life cannot be overstated. This is why we are encouraged over and over again in God's Word to do good works –

- Jesus encouraged us to shine before others through our good works (Matthew 5:16)

- We should do good works to prove our repentance before God (Acts 26:20)

- We should not repay anyone evil for evil, but do good to all (1 Thessalonians 5:15)

- We are encouraged not to grow weary in doing good works (2 Thessalonians 3:13)

- We should be 'rich' in good works, and the context is those whom God has blessed financially should be willing to share what they have with others (1 Timothy 6:18)
- We should show ourselves to have a patten of good works in all things (Titus 2:7)
- We should be ready for every good work (Titus 3:1)
- We should be careful to maintain our good works (Titus 3:8, 14)
- We should encourage each other to do good works (Hebrews 10:24)
- We should not forget to do good and share what we have with others, as this pleases God (Hebrews 13:16)

There are other reasons to do good works as well. One is that we can bring much glory to God by other people witnessing our good works and praising Him (1 Peter 2:12). This one has a caveat though. God's Word says do not let your right hand know what your left hand is doing when you are doing your good works (Matthew 6:3), meaning do not intentionally do your good works before others to garner the praise of other people; because if you do, that praise will be your only reward (Matthew 6:1-2). However, His Word also says that even the good works of people who are doing them in the right way (not to gain praise from people) cannot be hidden forever; and eventually will reveal themselves to others in due time (1 Timothy 5:25, NIV), bringing glory to God. The key is to make sure we are doing our good works for the right reasons.

God's Word also says that through the doing of good works believers can silence the foolish talk of ignorant people (1 Peter 2:15). There are many places in the Bible where God says those who claim to be wise really are not. Especially those who claim there is no God, those people are fools (Psalm 14:1). They cannot be wise, because if the fear of God is the beginning of wisdom (Proverbs 9:10), yet they say there is no God, then they certainly don't fear Him; so they cannot be wise, but rather ignorant. This means that anyone who teaches or professes evolution to explain how the universe and people came to be, rather than everything was created by God through Jesus (John 1:3), is speaking foolishly. And

Chapter 7: Do Good Works

God says they can be silenced by the believer's practice of doing good works because that could only come about (especially on the worldwide scale that it has) if God truly existed (3 John 11).

Now these are all very important reasons to do good works. They prove we have saving faith, they please God, they bring glory to God, and they silence foolish talk from those who think they are wise but are not. But there are a couple more reasons for doing good works that need to be brought up because these have to do with the *permanency* of a believer's good works; as well as the warnings for those who don't do good works.

First, God promises His rewards for a believer's good works are for all eternity (1 Peter 1:4). Did you know that? The Bible says that for those who do their good works in Christ, they will be rewarded by God the Father and Jesus for the doing of those good works…forever. Don't miss the amazing grace and graciousness of God in this. God will test us to make sure our faith in His Son Jesus is genuine, and we pass that test by the doing of good works, yet God will also reward those good works for all eternity, just like He rewarded Abraham for his (Genesis 15:16-18).

The idea of God rewarding people for believing in Him goes all the way back to a book in the Bible that was written before Genesis. It says in the book of Job that God repays a person according to their work, and gives a person a reward according to the way they live their life (Job 34:11). King David said surely there is a reward from God for a righteous person (Psalm 58:11) and the wisest man who ever lived, King Solomon, said he who sows righteousness (does good works in God) has a sure reward (Proverbs 11:18). We also see this promise in the Old Testament where it says the Lord God will come, and His reward is with Him (Isaiah 40:10). Jesus confirms this in the last chapter of the Bible by saying, *"Behold, I am coming quickly, and My reward is with Me, to give to everyone according to his work."* (Revelation 22:15)

Jesus often referred to this reward He is talking about as treasure in heaven (Matthew 19:21, Luke 12:33). No one is completely sure what that means, as there is nowhere in God's Word that says exactly what treasure in heaven is, but the Bible does give us some clues. We know it cannot be money because money is an earthly creation that God says will eventually be destroyed (Matthew 6:19), and a person cannot serve God and money anyway (Matthew 6:24, NIV), so why would God's treasure in heaven be money?

Could it be gold or silver, because Jesus said treasure in heaven will not be destroyed? (Matthew 6:20). Well, maybe. God says all the gold and silver in the world are His (Haggai 2:8), and if we are heirs with Christ in God then we are heirs to all that is His (Romans 8:17). However, God's Word also says gold and silver can rust (Matthew 6:19), so it doesn't seem likely that that would be it either.

The first mention of a reward in the Bible comes in Genesis where God said to Abram that He is his reward (15:1), So I believe it is more likely that God's final reward for believers comes out of a closeness with Him that cannot be obtained any other way than to be granted by Him through the redemption of our bodies. This redemption will give us the knowledge of God, because when our bodies are redeemed, we will be like Christ (1 John 3:2). Then, having this complete knowledge of God, it will allow us to fully love Him, and worship Him, and fellowship with Him in a way that will be so fulfilling and awesome that anything else will pale in comparison.

This doesn't mean God's reward couldn't also involve actual riches in some form, whether physical gold, silver and precious stones or something else entirely. We know we're going to be given a place to live in heaven (John 14:2). This is a physical reward in and of itself, and the New King James translation this book uses for most references from the Bible calls these places in which we will live mansions. We also know for some people the reward of God will involve participating in a hierarchy of authority and rule over others in His thousand-year kingdom on earth; involving things like governing cities (Luke 19:11-19). This authority and rule will begin with King David and work its way down from there (Jeremiah 30:9).

This seems appropriate, that David would be first. Not only did salvation for the world come through God's relationship with His people Israel (John 4:22), and David was the greatest king of Israel (2 Samuel 7:16, 25-16), but we see in the Psalms that David's relationship with God was by far and away the most important thing to Him. It seemed to reach a level that has never been achieved before or since, and is probably a big reason why God gave only to David the distinction of being called a man after God's own heart (Acts 13:22). I should also point out, though, that in that verse in Acts, God said David would *do* everything He wanted him to do, so that has to be another reason that David will be first in authority too.

Still, for many others, God's reward will also include some measure of authority and rule in His kingdom. And it would seem like along with a higher level of authority and rule would come with it a need for closer access to God to carry that out. This is starting to get into speculation on my part so I will stop there, but whatever the reward and treasure spoken of in God's Word consists of, it is going to be incredible, and God wants us to get excited about it (Hebrews 11:16).

Now, all these things are excellent reasons to do good works. But what about the places in God's Word where there are warnings for believers in Christ who don't do good works? There are several places in the Bible that talk about this, but there are two in particular I would like to bring to your attention. The first is found in the Gospel of John, chapter 15. Jesus had just told His disciples that anyone who has faith in Him will do the same things He has been doing (14:12). He also said three times that if anyone truly loves Him, they will obey His commandments (14:15, 21, 23), and added that he who does not truly love Him will not obey His commandments (14:24). He then followed this up with an illustration of how it all works.

> *"I am the true vine, and My Father is the vinedresser. Every branch in Me that does not bear fruit He takes away; and every branch that bears fruit He prunes, that it may bear more fruit...I am the vine, you are the branches. He who abides in Me, and I in him, bears much fruit; for without Me you can do nothing. If anyone does not abide in Me, he is cast out as a branch and is withered; and they gather them and throw them into the fire, and are burned." (15:1-2, 5-6)*

So what is Jesus saying here? Is he really saying every believer in Christ (those who are connected to Him through faith), that if they don't do good works then God will reject them? Well, we already know there is nothing we can do to save ourselves, that salvation is through faith in

Jesus alone, so wouldn't it make sense that if we *didn't* do anything but have faith in Jesus we should be ok? Well, not really. True faith will always produce good works. We already talked about that earlier in this chapter. But now is Jesus saying believers that don't produce good works will go to hell?

We will cover in detail in chapter 12 how faith and what Jesus commands us to do in and through faith go together; and whether a believer can really lose their salvation or not through disobedience. For now though, it seems pretty straightforward in verses five and six what we need to do in order to bear fruit (do good works) – we need to abide in Him. That word 'abide' means to remain, so we need to remain in Christ through faith in Him. This is a choice that we do not make only one time, we must choose to *remain* in Christ; and if we continue to do that, *we will* produce good works.

Now there will be some who say bearing fruit isn't only talking about good works, and that is correct. Some of the fruit of the Spirit is said to be love, joy, peace, patience, kindness, goodness, gentleness, faithfulness and self-control (Galatians 5:22), and there is other fruit of the Spirit as well (2 Corinthians 9:6-15, Ephesians 5:9, James 3:17-18). However, most of these fruits are displayed through the doing of good works towards God and others. So to say that one can be a true Christian, yet not have any good works, is incorrect according to what Jesus says in John 15.

If there is still any reason for doubt that believers in Christ must do good works, in Jesus' seven letters to the churches in Revelation, He talks extensively about the good works those churches are doing (or in this case not doing). For those churches not doing good works, Jesus calls them either dead, or warns them that if they don't start doing good works He will punish them (Revelation 2:5, 3:3, 16-18).

Here are some of the things Jesus said about good works (or lack thereof) to the churches, and these are just as relevant to us today as they were to those churches then –

- *"I know your (good) works, your labor, your patience, and that you cannot bear those who are evil."* (Revelation 2:2a, word

Chapter 7: Do Good Works

added in parenthesis for clarification, and applies to any reference to works in the letters to the seven churches)

- *"I know your works, tribulation and poverty..."* (2:9a)
- *"I know your works, and where you dwell, where Satan's throne is."* (2:13a)
- *"I know your works, love, service, faith and your patience; and as for your works, the last are more than the first."* (2:19)
- *"I know all the things you do, and that you have a reputation for being alive – but you are dead. Wake up! Strengthen what little (good work) remains, for even what is left is almost dead. I find that your actions do not meet the requirements of My God...Yet there are a few people in the church in Sardis who have not soiled their clothes with evil. They will walk with Me in white for they are worthy."* (3:1b-2, 4, NLT, words in parenthesis added for clarification)
- *"I know your works. See, I have set before you an open door, and no one can shut it; for you have a little strength, have kept My Word, and have not denied My name."* (3:8)
- *"I know your works, that you are neither cold nor hot."* (3:15a)

Seven letters to the churches and in each one Jesus begins by telling them He knows of their good works, or lack thereof. Jesus would not begin each letter the same way if good works were not something that was so important to Him. Good works confirm that our faith in Christ is genuine, so it would make sense that good works would take such a high priority in His letters to the churches.

We also see that Jesus confirms what we originally saw from the book of James, that a faith that doesn't have good works is a dead faith and cannot save anyone. Jesus illustrated this before when He said He is the vine and believers are the branches, and any believer that doesn't produce good works will be removed and thrown into the fire of hell (because a lack of good works means their faith is dead). His letter now to the church in Sardis makes this crystal clear.

He calls that church dead because the believers among them are doing very few good works. Jesus then goes on to single out the ones that still are doing good works and says those people will be saved (walk with Him in white clothes). This implies everyone else, because of their lack of good works, will not. And in case there is any confusion about that, Jesus says in the next verse that those clothed in white garments will not have their name blotted out of the Book of Life (3:5). This letter that Jesus is sending to the church at Sardis confirms that not only is faith in Him without good works a dead faith that cannot save anyone, but it *is* also possible for a person to go from a state of salvation to one who is not saved (being blotted out of the Book of Life).

Again, we will discuss that last point in detail in chapter 12, but it should be very clear to you now how important it is for a believer to do good works. The apostle Paul understood this and taught it often in his epistles. Seven of the ten examples of encouragements for believers to do good works given earlier in this chapter came from Paul. He even went so far as to say a so- called believing widow who did not show herself to do many good works should not be taken into the church; because she was 'dead while she lives' (1 Timothy 5:5-6, 10-11). This example can only mean Paul considers anyone who claims to know Christ, yet have no good works, to not really have the Holy Spirit living inside them, because they do not have true saving faith.

Let's move on to the next step and see how giving is also such an integral part of being a believer in Christ, and will also be necessary in order to hear, "Well done, good and faithful servant."

Chapter 8

Give

The subject of giving what one has back to God, or to someone else, runs throughout the entire Bible. The first time we read of giving is early on in Genesis when Cain and Abel brought offerings to the Lord (Genesis 4:3-4) and the last time is in Revelation after eternity has begun and all the nations will bring gifts to God at New Jerusalem (Revelation 21:24-26). In the Old Testament we see things like Abraham giving a tenth of all he has to Melchizedek, priest of the Most High God. Who was the forerunner to Christ, without father and mother and made like the Son of God (Hebrews 7:3). God's commandment for the Israelites to give a tenth of everything they have to the Lord (Leviticus 27:30) ; and a warning that those who do not follow the command to tithe are robbing God (Malachi 3:8).

In the New Testament we see things like Jesus telling the Jewish leaders who were in opposition to Him, that even though they don't practice what they preach, at least they were correct in giving a tenth of all they had to God (Matthew 23:23). To what God's perfect ideal for the church should be. That no believer should ever be in need because every believer should share all they have with each other (Acts 4:32-35). We will come back to that in more detail a bit later, but for now we should first ask the question – Why must we give?

Ultimately, we must give because God is a giver. He made everything in the universe for the main purpose of *giving* life to humanity, to you and to me. We must not overlook this fact. Everything you see and read and learn about the earth, moon, and stars, about the universe and how it all works together, was done by God in preparation for His greatest creation – people made in His image (Genesis 1:26-29). Remember, it was only *after* God created the first person that He called His creation 'very good' (verse 31). God made the universe so big that even with incredibly powerful telescopes we still cannot count how many stars there are; and He made it so complex that we still don't understand things like where gravity really comes from. Yet after God made all that, He only called it 'good' until He made the first person in His image. Then He called it all 'very good.'

This universe God made to support life for humanity, for you and for me, He sustains constantly (Hebrews 1:3). God also sustains the very breaths we take each and every day (Job 34:14-15). So God continues to give to us at all times; and our response to how much God has given us, and continues to give us, should be that we give back in return. First to God, and then to each other. However, even though the main reason why we should give is because God is a giver, there are also many more reasons why we should give as well.

We should give because it teaches us to fear the Lord –

We give first because God is a giver, yes, but right up there in importance is this other reason for us to give; because the Bible says giving of a tenth of all we have back to God teaches us to fear Him (Deuteronomy 14:22-23). In the introduction, I stated that the church has lost its fear of God and the main proof of that is how few people there are in the church that actually tithe back to God. I have seen many statistics on this, and they range from less than ten percent to less than twenty; but most times they say only 10-15% of believers give a tenth of 'all their increase' (verse 22).

Now there are those who say tithing was given through the law and because believers in Christ are not under the law (Galatians 5:18), then tithing doesn't apply to the church. To those who believe that, I would say two things. First, tithing began before the law was given as we saw in the example of Abraham giving a tenth of everything he had to Melchizedek. God's Word says Melchizedek was a kind of forerunner to Christ in the flesh (Hebrews 7:1-6). So, we have the example of someone who was saved through faith, to whom all other believers since that time are connected (Romans 4:16), who tithed to a type of Christ. Therefore, tithing to Christ (God) should continue for believers who are not under the law.

Chapter 8: Give

Second, if you still want to say that example doesn't apply to the church, then I say fine. Let's remove any particular number and go by what the Bible also says. That to those whom God has given much, then much more will be required of them in terms contributing back to God's kingdom (Luke 19:15-26). I can assure you this means *more* than ten percent. When you combine that with the fact that by the world's standards (and probably God's standards as well) that almost everyone in the United States would be considered 'those whom God has given much,' then most believers in the church in America should be giving more than ten percent of what they have back to God, and to others.

Oh, now you want to go back to the first example and make the benchmark for giving only ten percent? Too late. But giving isn't supposed to be a burden God gives us. Giving is supposed to be something we get to do out of thanksgiving to God that brings much glory to Him; and giving has many blessings associated with it.

We should give out of thanksgiving because everything comes from God –

God's Word says that everything a person has comes from Him (1 Chronicles 29:14a), and the reason this is so is because God gives a person the ability to produce wealth (Deuteronomy 8:18). There are other factors that make the statement that everything a person has comes from God true as well. God could direct a person's interests growing up into a particular field of work, or into a certain school, or into this job or that. But the main reason everything comes from God is He created people to be able to work. He gives them all their skills required to work and thus receive an income, so everything a person has comes from Him.

This is true for everyone, whether a believer in Christ or not. The difference is for those who recognize that everything they have comes from God, it turns the word 'have' into 'received.' Once a person recognizes they have received everything from God, it is then that a person can begin to give back to God and others out of thanksgiving for what they have *received* from Him. And it is also at that point that certain verses from God's Word will make more sense, such as *"We have given You only what comes from Your hand."* (1 Chronicles 29:14b, NIV). So, we recognize that we have freely received, and that we should freely give in return (Matthew 10:8). When we do this, we are giving in the right way. Not out of reluctance or compulsion, rather from a thankful heart, and this pleases God (2 Corinthians 9:7). His Word says when we give this way God accepts the gift, because it was given willingly (2 Corinthians 8:12).

We should also give because of the blessings that come along with it. The Bible talks about many promises of blessings that go along with giving -

- Whatever we give to the Lord is considered holy by Him (Leviticus 27:9)

- Those who give to the poor all over the world, their righteousness will endure forever (Psalm 112:9, NIV)

- When we give to the poor, we lend to the Lord (Proverbs 19:17)

- Whoever gives to the poor will not lack anything (Proverbs 28:27)

- When we give a tithe to God, He promises to pour out His blessings on us (Malachi 3:10)

- When we give, we store up treasure for ourselves in heaven (Matthew 6:20)

- When we give, God will take it, add more to it, and will give it back to us (Luke 6:38)

- Our giving to the poor will be repaid to us when we are resurrected (Luke 14:14)

- Our giving on earth will gain friends for us in heaven (Luke 16:9)

- Our giving is credited to our account in heaven (Philippians 4:17)

These are promises given by God, who cannot lie (Titus 1:2), for whom it is impossible to lie (Hebrews 6:18); and because of the surety of these promises and more, God says it is ok to test Him in our giving (Malachi 3:10). This is the only time in Scripture where we are given permission to test the Lord our God, so that He can prove the promises written in the Bible about giving are true.

We should give because of the warnings to those who do not –

Chapter 8: Give

As many blessings as there are in God's Word for those who give, there are even more warnings for those who do not. This is probably because the love of money is the root of all kinds of evil (1 Timothy 6:10), and God knew how much pain and suffering were going to be caused in the world over people's insatiable desire to get more and more of it (Ecclesiastes 5:10).

- Do not work too hard to be rich, for riches can be lost very quickly (Proverbs 23:5)
- Jesus said wherever a person's treasure is (if it's their wealth), then their heart will be there also (and not with God) (Matthew 6:21)
- Jesus said a person cannot serve God and money, because they will be loyal to one and despise the other (Matthew 6:24, NIV)
- Jesus said woe to the rich, for they have already received their comfort (Luke 6:24)
- Jesus said those who are not trustworthy with money cannot be trusted with heavenly riches (Luke 16:11)
- Jesus said it is hard for a rich person to enter into heaven (be saved) (Luke 18:24)
- Those who give little will receive little in return (2 Corinthians 9:6)
- Believers who love money have strayed from the faith (1 Timothy 6:10)
- Believers are told to flee from the love of money and from greed (1 Timothy 6:11)
- For those who store up wealth for themselves it will be used as a witness against them at the final judgment (James 5:3)
- Greed is seen as idolatry by God (Colossians 3:5)

- If a believer has enough money to live well and will not share it with other believers who are in need, the love of God does not abide in that person (1 John 3:17)

These are some pretty stern warnings from God for those who store up wealth for themselves and are not rich toward God and other people in their giving.

I would like to point out a few things though. First, even though many of these warnings seem to imply a rich person will most likely not be someone who is a believer in Christ, because of reasons like pride and that you cannot serve both God and money. There is nothing inherently wrong with being rich. God blessed the kings of Israel with incredible wealth, including king David who will be second in command beneath Jesus during His thousand-year reign on earth. So having riches does not exclude a person from being saved. Rather, it's the fact that most people with a lot of wealth trust in their riches instead of God (Proverbs 18:11); and because of that, they are not able to humble themselves to come to the point of repentance to salvation (2 Timothy 2:25).

Second, and this is for the believer. Did you notice that God's Word says believers who love money have strayed from the faith? The Greek word for strayed is apoplanao (ap-op-lan-ah-o) and it means to wander away from the truth. So, what the apostle Paul is literally saying is believers who love money have wandered away from the truth of the gospel, salvation by grace through faith in Christ. This is alarming considering the parable where Jesus said when one of His sheep wanders away from Him, that sheep is lost, and will require Jesus to go look for that person and bring them back to salvation through faith (Luke 15:4-7). We will talk extensively in chapter 12 about the many examples from God's Word that seem to indicate believers can walk away from their faith to the point of losing their salvation.

We should give because it is a powerful witness of God's grace to the world when believers share all they have with one another –

In Acts, chapter 4 we find the ideal for the church in how we should give. This is probably one of the most challenging parts of God's Word found anywhere in the Bible. There are many truths Christianity teaches that get unbelievers worked up into a tizzy. At the top of that list is the truth that there is only one way to be saved from eternal punishment in the lake of fire, and that is by God's saving grace through faith in Jesus Christ. However, if you want a truth from the Bible that gets most Christians worked up into a tizzy, it is the fact that God wants us to share all that we have with each other so that there will be no believer who is in need.

> *"All the believers were united in heart and mind. And they felt that what they owned was not their own, so they shared everything they had. The apostles testified powerfully to the resurrection of the Lord Jesus, and God's great blessing was upon them all. There were no needy people among them, because those who owned land or houses would sell them and bring the money to the apostles to give to those in need." – Acts 4:32-35, NLT*

This is the kind of witness the church should be doing in a time like today. I realize there are places in the world where one cannot make it known that they are a Christian or they will be killed, so opportunities to share are limited. But what if in countries where that was not the case, like the United States (not yet anyway*), if the church actually began to live like this? Can you imagine what would happen? I will tell you what would happen. The country would experience it's third Great Awakening where millions upon millions of unsaved people would be drawn to the truth of salvation through faith in Jesus alone. That's what would happen. Sadly, this will not come to pass because the church is so weak, but that doesn't mean we cannot take a look at this example and use it as inspiration to share more than we normally would with our brothers and sisters in the faith. This still brings glory to God, and for those who do, He will use it to bless both you and those around you.

We should give because God gave Himself –

Earlier in this chapter it was said that, ultimately, we must give because God is a giver, that He continues to give to us at all times, and our response to all these gifts from God should be for us to give back in return. Some examples of God's gifts were given, but you might have noticed His biggest gift was not mentioned until now, and that is the gift of Himself.

Not only did God create everything in the universe for the purpose of sustaining the lives of all the people He was going to create in His image, but He did all this knowing beforehand that it would also require Him to sacrifice Himself (2 Timothy 1:9, NLT). God knew before He laid the foundation of the earth that to create everything, including people made in His image, was going to eventually require Him to become flesh in the person of Jesus Christ, and allow the people He created to kill Him on a cross. All in order to make everything work out in the end for those who would believe in Him (Matthew 20:28). He knew all this before He created anything, yet He did it anyway; and His Word says He did it for you and for me (Galatians 2:20).

If that doesn't make you want to give back to God, and to others, I don't know what will. Hopefully, it will do for you what it does for me and make you feel like no matter how much you give it's not enough compared to what God has already given you. If that is the case for you, then you're probably ready to tackle an art of giving that rarely gets talked about, but it's there in God's Word, and no discussion about giving is complete without it.

Hilarious giving –

There is a Greek word from 2 Corinthians 9:7 that is not translated properly into any English version of the Bible that I'm aware of. This is a shame because the correct translation changes the meaning of what is being said completely. The apostle Paul takes quite a bit of time in his second letter to the Corinthian church to talk about giving, how it should be done, and has this to say about giving –

> *"Each one of you should give what you have decided to give in your heart, not reluctantly or under compulsion, for God loves a cheerful giver." – 2 Corinthians 9:7, NIV*

The word 'cheerful' is hilaros in the Greek, from where we get the word hilarious. So what Paul is really saying here is God loves a *hilarious* giver. That's quite a different statement than saying God loves a cheerful giver. Yes, we are supposed to give willingly. God's Word says gifts given willingly are accepted by Him (2 Corinthians 8:12). However, Paul isn't saying God loves someone who gives willingly; we are all supposed to do that. Paul is saying God loves someone who gives liberally to all (2 Corinthians 9:13). And the verse right after that says for anyone who becomes a hilarious giver, God will make sure you have all that you need to do so (verse 8).

Now, there are a few other things that need to be said about hilarious giving. First, hilarious giving for Christ is an absolute indication of a faith that saves. We have a wonderful example of this from God's Word in the story of Zacchaeus. Jesus came to the city of Jericho and there was a tax collector there by the name of Zacchaeus. Jesus called him by name and said He must be a visitor at Zacchaeus' house. Zacchaeus was so moved by Jesus' recognition of him that he pledged to give half of his possessions to the poor, and also said if he took anything in taxes from someone that they did not owe, he would pay them back four times as much (Luke 19:8). Jesus' response to these words were, *"Today salvation has come to this house"* (verse 9).

Now you can try to spin that any way you want, but a literal interpretation of what Jesus said is, because you have committed to do this, you are demonstrating you are a person who is saved through your faith in Me. Zacchaeus' action of hilarious giving proved he believed in Jesus and Jesus said it resulted in the salvation of his soul.

The second thing that needs to be pointed out is hilarious giving doesn't have to involve a large quantity of money or possessions. We have another wonderful story of the poor widow who Jesus singled out to prove that you don't have to give a lot to be a hilarious giver. During Jesus' last visit to Jerusalem before He would be crucified, He sat in front of the temple treasury and watched many people put in large sums of money in their offerings to God. Then a widow came and put in what are described as two small copper coins (Mark 12:42). They were called mites and were the smallest form of money there was at the time.

Jesus called His disciples together because He didn't want them to miss what just happened and said the widow gave more to God than all the others because she gave everything she had while the others gave out of their wealth (verses 43-44). This shows one does not have to give a large amount of money to be considered a hilarious giver. Rather, when one gives over and above what God expects of them, it is the same kind of hilarious giving that God loves to see.

So, to sum up, believers in Christ are supposed to be givers because God is such a wonderful giver Himself. He gave us the universe and everything in it to sustain us. He gave us life; He gives us everything we have in this world, and He gave us a way to be reconciled to Him through faith in Jesus' life, death and resurrection. Yes, the benchmark for a believer's giving is set pretty high, considering nothing our own and sharing everything we have with each other in the church. But even though it's very rare to find a believer today that does this, for those that do give generously, it still demonstrates that they do not hope in riches but in God (1 Timothy 6:17-18); and God promises to bless both the gifts and the givers of the gifts themselves beyond measure, both in this life and in the eternal life to come.

Chapter 9

Be a Good Manager of What You Have Received

In the last chapter, it was mentioned that for those who recognize everything they have comes from God, it changes the word 'have' into 'received,' because they acknowledge the fact that they are receivers from God for what He gives them. This understanding is a big step in the process that enables believers to willingly and generously give back to God and to others. The next step in this process is to understand that everything we receive from God isn't really ours. Even after we have received it, it still belongs to God (Psalm 24:1, NIV). This ultimately makes us *managers* of what we have received from God; and as managers of God's things, we will certainly have to be a good one if we want to hear, "Well done, good and faithful servant," when we meet Jesus for the first time.

Now everything we have received from God isn't summed up in only wealth. Remember, people are given a certain skill set from God (Exodus 35:30-35) that allows them to produce wealth (Deuteronomy 8:17-18). This allows us to receive the rewards of those skills (our income). However, it goes much farther than that. We also received our body from God, who knit us together in our mother's womb (Psalm 139:13, NIV). For those born in America we received the gift of being able to live in the greatest country the world has ever known; and for believers born in the last fifty years or so, we also received the gift of possibly not seeing death before Jesus comes back again.*

There are many other examples that could be given for what we have received from God. However, for this step of being a good manager I would like to focus on two, since God's Word seems to talk a lot about both of them. The first *is* the wealth that we have received from God; as managing wealth involves a lot more than just giving a certain percentage of it back to God and to others. The second is managing something very important that every believer has also been given by God – spiritual gifts from the Holy Spirit (Romans 12, 1 Corinthians 12, Ephesians 4).

Any discussion about managing the wealth we have received from God needs to go deeper than just giving some of it back to Him and others, because the parables God gives for managing wealth go much deeper than that. There are several parables to choose from, but two stand out as the best examples of how God expects us to be good managers of what we receive from Him; and that He will reward the good managers, but punish the poor ones.

The first one is the parable of the talents.

> *"For the kingdom of heaven is like a man traveling to a far country, who called his own servants and delivered his goods to them. And to one he gave five talents, to another two, and to another one, to each according to his own ability; and immediately he went on a journey. Then he who had received the five talents went and traded with them, and made another five talents. And likewise he who had received two gained two more also. But he who had received one went and dug in the ground, and hid his lord's money. After a long time the lord of those servants came and settled accounts with them."*

> *"So he who had received five talents came and brought five other talents, saying, 'Lord, you delivered to me five talents; look, I have gained five more talents besides them.' His lord said to him, 'Well done, good and faithful servant; you were faithful over a few things, I will make you ruler over many things. Enter into the joy of your lord.' He also who had received two talents came and said, 'Lord, you delivered to me two talents; look, I have gained two more talents besides them.' His lord said to him, 'Well done, good and faithful servant; you have been faithful over a few things, I will make you ruler over many things. Enter into the joy of your lord.'*

Chapter 9: Be a Good Manager of What You Have Received

> *"Then he who had received the one talent came and said, 'Lord, I knew you to be a hard man, reaping where you have not sown, and gathering where you have not scattered seed. And I was afraid, and went and hid your talent in the ground. Look, there you have what is yours.' But his lord answered and said to him, 'You wicked and lazy servant, you knew that I reap where I have not sown, and gather where I have not scattered seed.'*
>
> *'So you ought to have deposited my money with the bankers, and at my coming I would have received back my own with interest. So take the talent from him, and give it to him who has ten talents. For to everyone who has, more will be given, and he will have abundance; but from him who does not have, even what he has will be taken away. And cast the unprofitable servant into the outer darkness. There will be weeping and gnashing of teeth.'" – Matthew 25:14-30*

So let's point out a few things here. First, it's obvious the man Jesus was talking about that went to a far country was Himself; and the far country He went to was heaven when He returned there after He was raised from the dead. The parable says He gave what was His to His servants, and that even while they were in possession of what He gave them, it was still considered His (verse 18). We already acknowledged that everything we receive from God is still His, and this parable confirms that.

From there we see Jesus expects us to manage well what He has given us while He resides in heaven, until He comes again (or we go to meet Him after death). For the two servants that did a good job, they were commended with the words of what this book is all about – hearing, "Well done, good and faithful servant." They heard those words and were greatly rewarded for their faithfulness and hard work while their master was gone.

For the servant that did not manage well what he was given, he was called wicked and lazy. Those are strong words and they are an indication that for those who are thinking I'll just use God's grace to get into heaven but I don't really care to do all the other things that Jesus expects me to do, let this serve as a warning to you. Cheap grace, as that is called, doesn't appear to save anyone. Did you see what happened to that servant? He was thrown into outer darkness. I can assure you outer darkness is not heaven because weeping and gnashing of teeth is always equated in the Bible with going to hell (Matthew 8:12, 13:42, 50, 22:13, 24:51, 25:30).

This is another strong proof from God's Word that people can lose their salvation through disobedience because constant willful disobedience over a period of time will be taken as unbelief (no faith) by God (1 Samuel 15:23, AMP, Ephesians 5:3-7, Colossians 3:1-7, Hebrews 4:6-11). Again, we will cover this topic in detail in chapter 12, but we can't just pass over it here without acknowledging what happened to the unfaithful servant.

For now, what should be understood is what Jesus gave to each servant was more than just wealth, rather it encompasses everything that God gives us. How do we know this? A talent is a unit of measurement equaling roughly seventy-five pounds of whatever is associated with it. Most of the time in God's Word it is referring to an amount of silver and gold (1 Kings 9:14, 28, 10:10, 14, 16:24, 20:39, 2 Kings 5:22-23, 15:19, 18:14, 23:33) others times bronze or iron (1 Chronicles 29:7), and one time it even refers to the size of the hailstones God will send over the whole earth when He is pouring out His wrath on an unbelieving world (Revelation 16:21).

The point is, while a talent does usually refer to silver and gold, the amount that Jesus gives to each servant (even the servant who received only one talent) would be more money than most people make in a lifetime so the reference is obviously referring to more than just physical wealth. It is referring to everything God gives us, which in the Bible is sometimes called the riches of God (Ecclesiastes 5:18-19), or the riches of Christ (Ephesians 3:8). This would certainly include the skills God gives us to earn wealth, and the wealth that is earned over the course of our lifetimes. However, those riches also include things like God's grace (Ephesians 1:7), knowledge and wisdom (Romans 11:33), as well as the measure of faith that God has given each one of us (Romans 12:3).

Chapter 9: Be a Good Manager of What You Have Received

Remember in the parable it said each servant was given according to their ability? (verse 15). This is not referring to wealth at all, but rather a combination of the skills, knowledge and wisdom a person has, and in the context of a believer, it would also include the strength of their faith. All of these should be considered as things that make up part of the 'talents' that Jesus gives to believers.

Now the parable goes on to say the two servants 'traded' with what they were given and they made it grow. Yes, this means we are to take the material wealth God gives us and make good use of it, but it also means we are to 'trade' in the non-material things and grow them as well. We must grow in knowledge, understanding and wisdom of God by reading His Word daily, and grow up in our faith to be strong disciples of Christ.

For the material things God gives us, we must know and understand these truths found in God's Word, and wisely apply them to our lives –

- We must know that we cannot take the material wealth we receive from God with us when we die (1 Timothy 6:6-8), but if we give it for the purpose of growing the kingdom of God in this world, and to the poor, we can pay it forward to our accounts in heaven (Philippians 4:17)

- We must understand that the reason we work is not only to provide for ourselves and our families, but also to have something to give to others (Ephesians 4:28)

- We must know that for those who have been given a lot of material wealth in this world, God expects them to be generous in sharing it with other believers (1 Timothy 6:18)

- We must understand that anyone who has been given material wealth in this world, yet will not share with other believers, does *not* have the love of God in them (1 John 3:17)

- We must know that God's ideal for His people is to take turns caring for each other out of their abundance. For those who have wealth now may not have wealth later in life, and those that are being supported now by another's abundance may be the ones called upon later on to provide for the ones that were supporting ythem before (2 Corinthians 8:13-15)

- We must understand that if our giving to God is not costing us in other areas of our lives (making us cut back on things like size of houses, expensive cars, number of vacations, etc.) then we are not giving enough, because we should not give to God that which costs us nothing. (2 Samuel 24:24)

- We must know that we should count all things as a loss compared to knowing our Lord Jesus Christ, and that we should suffer the loss of them so we may gain eternal life through faith in Him (Philippians 3:7-8)

Believers must know and understand we are to give to God and others in these ways because our attitude should be the same as our Savior Jesus, who was rich beyond belief in heaven, yet for our sakes gave it all up and became poor (2 Corinthians 8:9).

Now the non-material things that God gives us through the indwelling of His Holy Spirit are more (and more important) than the wealth He gives us. Things like knowledge (2 Peter 1:3), understanding (Colossians 1:9), wisdom (Ephesians 1:17), faith (Galatians 5:5), hope (Romans 15:13), and love (2 Timothy 1:7). All these must also be increased (traded well) if we are to hear, "Well done, good and faithful servant," when our Master returns (or we return to Him). But there are also individual gifts given to every believer that must be traded well too.

There are twenty-six individual gifts of the Holy Spirit listed in the Old and New Testaments. God's Word says every believer has been given at least one of these (1 Corinthians 12:7), and some may receive more than one (12:31).

Here are the individual gifts of the Holy Spirit and where to find them in God's Word –

- Administration –   1 Corinthians 12:28
- Communication –   1 Peter 4:10-11
- Craftsmanship (skill with hands, includes music) – Exodus 31:3-6

Chapter 9: Be a Good Manager of What You Have Received

- Discernment – 1 Corinthians 12:10
- Encouragement – Romans 12:8
- Evangelism – Ephesians 4:11
- Faith – 1 Corinthians 12:9
- Giving – Romans 12:8
- Healing – 1 Corinthians 12:9, 28
- Helps – 1 Corinthians 12:28
- Hospitality – 1 Peter 4:9-10
- Intercession (praying for others) – 1 Timothy 2:1
- Interpretation – 1 Corinthians 12:30
- Interpretation of tongues – 1 Corinthians 12:10, 28
- Knowledge – 1 Corinthians 12:8
- Leadership – Romans 12:8
- Mercy – Romans 12:8
- Miracles – 1 Corinthians 12:10, 28
- Pastoring – Ephesians 4:11
- Preaching 1 Peter 4:11
- Prophecy – Romans 12:6, 1 Corinthians 12:10, 28, Ephesians 4:11
- Serving – Romans 12:7, Ephesians 4:11, 1 Peter 4:11
- Strenghth – Judges 14:6, 19, 15:14, 16:28
- Teaching – Romans 12:7, 1 Corinthians 12:28, Ephesians 4:11
- Speaking in tongues – 1 Corinthians 12:10, 28
- Wisdom – 1 Corinthians 12:8

This is a big list, and we don't have space in this book to go over each one of them, but I would encourage you to read each of these sections of

Scripture to gain insights about these gifts. We can, however, take some time to point out a few things about individual gifts from the Holy Spirit.

First, you may have noticed that some of these gifts are things that the Spirit gives to all believers, and that is correct. Every believer receives faith from the Spirit, every believer receives knowledge of God from the Spirit, and every believer receives wisdom from the Spirit. But there are others on this list that I would argue all believers also receive in at least some measure from the Holy Spirit as well. Things like discernment, encouragement, evangelism, giving, helps, hospitality, intercession, mercy and serving. There are places in God's Word where *every* believer is called to practice those things. And He would not command every believer to do all those things unless He first gave us the ability, through the Spirit, to do them.

However, if a believer receives an *individual* gift of faith, knowledge, wisdom or any of the other gifts mentioned in God's Word, then they have received an *extra* measure of those things above and beyond what most believers have; and these gifts were given for specific tasks that God has for each of those believers to perform within the body of Christ.

Now every believer should try to find what their individual gift(s) are that they have been given by the Holy Spirit (Ephesians 5:17). This is because the gifts were given by God for the building up of the body of Christ, His church. In order that that the church would grow, and all believers would come to maturity and oneness in the faith and knowledge of Jesus (Ephesians 4:11-16). We are told that God gave these individual gifts according to His will (Hebrews 2:4), and that we must use them (1 Peter 4:10), and not neglect them (1 Timothy 4:14). We are also told we should eagerly desire these individual spiritual gifts and ask God to give us more of them (1 Corinthians 14:1).

So, getting back to our parable, we see that if we manage well the 'talents' that we are given, then we can expect to hear, "Well done, good and faithful servant," and we will be rewarded greatly by our Lord and Savior Jesus (verses 21 and 23). We also see if a believer does not manage well the 'talent' that they are given…well, let's leave the rest of that for chapter 12.

Chapter 9: Be a Good Manager of What You Have Received

However, I did say there were two parables that showed God expects us to manage well what we have been given, and the second one is the parable of the shrewd manager – Jesus told his disciples:

"There was a rich man whose manager was accused of wasting his possessions. So he called him in and asked him, 'What is this I hear about you? Give an account of your management, because you cannot be manager any longer.'

"The manager said to himself, 'What shall I do now? My master is taking away my job. I'm not strong enough to dig, and I'm ashamed to beg— I know what I'll do so that, when I lose my job here, people will welcome me into their houses.'

"So he called in each one of his master's debtors. He asked the first, 'How much do you owe my master?' "'Nine hundred gallons of olive oil,' he replied. "The manager told him, 'Take your bill, sit down quickly, and make it four hundred and fifty.' "Then he asked the second, 'And how much do you owe?' "'A thousand bushels of wheat,' he replied. "He told him, 'Take your bill and make it eight hundred.'

"The master commended the dishonest manager because he had acted shrewdly. For the people of this world are more shrewd in dealing with their own kind than are the people of the light. I tell you, use worldly wealth to gain friends for yourselves, so that when it is gone, you will be welcomed into eternal dwellings."

"Whoever can be trusted with very little can also be trusted with much, and whoever is dishonest with very little will also be dishonest with much. So if you have not been trustworthy in handling worldly wealth, who will trust you with true riches? And if you have not been trustworthy with someone else's property, who will give you property of your own?" – Luke 16:1-12, NIV

Let's go through this parable just like we did with the parable of the talents and see what it is saying.

Jesus is the rich man and the manager was a believer. He had to have been a believer because only a believer would be given any of the riches of Christ, and he even called Jesus his Master. The manager was wasting what he was given, so Jesus was going to take it away from him; but before he lost his job, he made sure other people would help him by reducing what they owed. This was essentially stealing from Jesus but, surprisingly, Jesus commended the manager for acting shrewdly and then opines about how He wishes His believers acted more shrewdly with the wealth they've been given to manage in this world.

Then Jesus acts shrewdly by taking what was a dishonest act and turning it around to show believers how they can benefit from what just happened. He said believers should take note and be shrewd with the wealth they have (share with other believers) so that they will also be welcomed into their homes in heaven when their worldly wealth is gone. Great advice! He then goes on to summarize that those who can be trusted with a little (worldly wealth), can be trusted with much (heavenly riches).

There are three other things I want to point out; consistencies between the two parables we looked at that you might have missed. First, one of the people in each parable went from a state of being considered a servant of Christ (which means saved) to losing their salvation through their disobedience. In the first parable that was obvious, that servant was thrown into outer darkness where there was weeping and gnashing of teeth. In this parable it's more subtle, but the outcome is the same.

Jesus was taking away his job, he could not be manager of His things anymore. That in and of itself isn't completely clear, but the next statement is. Jesus said that manager acted shrewdly with 'his own kind' and separated him from people 'of the light.' *That* message is clear, he lost his salvation through his disobedience, which ultimately is seen as a lack of faith by God.

The second thing to point out is how believers manage what we are given by Jesus now (worldly wealth and other gifts of the Spirit) will make a big difference in how they will spend eternity in heaven. In the first parable we saw that when the two servants managed well what they were given, they received substantially more for all eternity. In the second parable the same is implied in that, if we manage well the little things we

Chapter 9: Be a Good Manager of What You Have Received

have been given on this earth, we will receive 'much' in heaven; which are the *true* riches that God wanted us to have all along.

And finally, to bring this chapter full circle. We said in the beginning everything we have received from God in this world (and I mean everything) is His, and we are simply managers of it all. This is the reason why we must manage well what we have received if we are to hear, "Well done, good and faithful servant," when we meet Jesus for the first time. However, at the end of this second parable, we see a change. In heaven we will no longer be managers of what we have received, rather we will be given that which is called our own. Sound exciting? Let's see what else we need to do to hear those words from Jesus, and to receive that which will be our own in heaven.

Well Done, Good and Faithful Servant

Chapter 10

Come Out of the World and Be Separate

I mentioned early on in the book that the steps didn't initially seem, to me anyway, to be in any particular order other than the first two. It will definitely be impossible to hear, "Well done, good and faithful servant," if a person is not a true believer in Christ (step 1) and also if a person who claims to be a believer continues to be a slave to sin and not turn from it (step 2). Then, I mentioned that as I actually began writing out the steps, I saw how they did tend to be more in a logical order than I thought. The reason being that one step builds upon the next, and it would be hard to do some of the later steps if a person did not do the ones before them first.

My thoughts on this have only become stronger as I progress through writing out each step. We must know our Master's business by staying in the Word of God everyday (step 3) if we are going to have any chance to live our lives as a sacrifice to God (step 4). We must stay connected to God through prayer (step 5) if we are going to have the love of God work through us in order to love one another (step 6). It is then out of love for God and others that we produce many good works (step 7); being generous in our giving because God has first given so much to us (step 8). All these then work together so that we manage well the material and non-material things given to us from God (step 9).

This next step of separating oneself from the world builds upon the steps before it; and is not, in my opinion, something that can be done (certainly not done well) if a person isn't already practicing the nine steps that come before it. This presents a big challenge though because if you recall from the introduction, the majority of believers in the church are not practicing most of the steps before this one. So then, how many in the church today have come out from the world and are separate? Not many. This is one of the main reasons why the church has become so weak.

Believers have definitely been commanded to come out from the world and be separate from it (2 Corinthians 6:17). However, most believers don't understand the reasons behind that command, and they are many.

First of all, we must understand that the majority of time we see the word 'world' in the Bible (and certainly when we see it in the New Testament), it is referring to everything and everyone who is against God. We see this clearly in the verses leading up to God's command to come out and be separate –

> *"Do not team up with those who are unbelievers. How can righteousness be a partner with wickedness? How can light live with darkness? What harmony can there be between Christ and the devil? How can a believer be a partner with an unbeliever? And what union can there be between God's temple and idols? For we are the temple of the living God. As God has said, 'I will live in them and walk among them. I will be their God and they will be my people. Therefore, come out from among unbelievers (the world), and separate yourselves from them, says the Lord.'"*
> *– 2 Corinthians 6:14-17a, NLT (words in parenthesis added)*

I hope reading that sent a chill through your body; it did for me to read it. God is very serious about His believers coming out and being separate from the world.

Throughout the first nine steps of this book, it should apparent by now that believers in Christ are different, very different, from non-believers. If you haven't grasped that fact by now, please take a moment to stop and consider how different we are. First of all, we are alive, not dead (Ephesians 2:1-5). We are free from the bondage of sin, not slaves to it (Romans 6:6). We are lights to a dark world (Philippians 2:15). We are children of God (John 1:2), not children of the devil (John 8:44). We call Jesus our Lord through His Holy Spirit inside us (1 Corinthians 12:3), and we have an inheritance in heaven waiting for us when we get there (1 Peter 1:4).

All these things make believers *very* different from non-believers. And when you add more things like believers are servants of God, managing His things, living their lives for Him, praying, loving God and others deeply, doing many good works and giving, the gap between a believer

Chapter 10: Come Out of the World and Be Separate

and a non-believer is so wide, it is like the chasm between heaven and hell that is so big it is impossible for anyone to cross (Luke 16:26).

If that isn't enough reasons to come out and be separate, consider the fact that Jesus said the world hates Him (John 7:7); and since the world hates Him, it will hate those who believe in Him (John 15:18). So now, with all this in mind, go back and read God's command again to come out of the world and be separate. Does it make a lot more sense now why believers in Christ need to separate themselves from the world?

So how do we do that? Do we cut ourselves off from everything and everyone who is not like us and live our lives in a bubble until Jesus returns or we go to Him? Well, no. We don't because God's Word says it's impossible to do that or we would have to leave this world (1 Corinthians 5:10), but also because that is not why we have been called out of the darkness of the world. We have been called by God to live *in* this world (John 17:11), even though we are not part of it (17:14), just as Jesus lived in the world but was not part of it (17:16).

Ok…so…how do we do that?

Well, making a pattern of consistently doing the first nine steps outlined in this book will go a long way towards being able to live in the world without being a part of it; but God's Word shows us there are more ways to do this as well which haven't been discussed yet.

Live as a soldier of Christ –

The idea of Christians being soldiers for Christ can teach us much about how believers are to live separate from the world. First of all, this is not an analogy, we are soldiers of Christ. God's Word says believers have been enlisted by Jesus as soldiers (2 Timothy 2:4), and the apostle Paul twice referred to other believers as 'fellow soldiers' (Philippians 2:25, Philemon 1:2). This fact means there are several things that must be considered.

- In some countries a person can decide for themselves if they want to be a soldier or not, and in other countries it is required. God's Word says Jesus chose certain people to be soldiers for Him (John 15:19)
- Soldiers are constantly training to be prepared for whatever they may be called upon to do. Christian soldiers need to always be

training to prepare for whatever God calls them to do (1 Peter 3:15)
- Soldiers have equipment they use to carry out the tasks they are ordered to do, and so do soldiers of Christ (Ephesians 6:11-17)
- Soldiers do not get caught up in civilian affairs when they are on duty or engaged in warfare. The Bible says the same thing about Christian soldiers (2 Timothy 2:4); and we are always on duty (1 Peter 3:15)
- Soldiers carry out what they are ordered to do, and they are punished when they don't. God's Word says He punishes His soldiers when they don't do what they are supposed to do (Hebrews 12:6-11)
- Soldiers assemble together to increase the amount of force they can bring to a fight. Christian soldiers need to assemble to increase the force they can bring against the principalities of this world (Ephesians 6:12)
- Soldiers stand up and fight for those who cannot fight for themselves. Soldiers of Christ are called to stand up to injustice, and to help those who cannot help themselves (Jeremiah 22:16)
- Soldiers are united against their enemies. Christian soldiers are united against our enemy, Satan (1 Peter 5:8)
- Many soldiers have families, but the orders of their commanding officer take precedent over their families. It is no different with soldiers of Christ. Jesus expects us to put Him (and His orders) before our families (Matthew 10:37)
- Soldiers stand out in any setting when in uniform. Soldiers of Christ stand out in their uniform of 'light' in a dark world (Matthew 5:14-16)

These are all things that illustrate how a soldier's life in this world is the same as being a soldier for Christ; but there is something else that needs to be pointed out as well.

When a soldier signs up for the military, he or she is locked into service for a specified amount of time. They cannot change their mind later and decide they no longer want to be a part of it. They are committed until

Chapter 10: Come Out of the World and Be Separate

their time is up, and it is the same with soldiers of Christ. When we come to salvation by God's grace through faith in our commanding officer Jesus, we are locked into a lifetime of service.

There is one difference though...kind of. In the military, if someone decides they have had enough and don't want to be a part of it anymore, they can 'walk away,' and spend the rest of the time of their commitment in prison (or in communist countries probably killed). However, if a Christian decides to walk away from their faith, they won't necessarily spend time in prison right away (although they will be putting themselves back in 'prison' in the world - Galatians 4:3), but God's Word indicates they will spend time in the prison of hell when they die (chapter 12).

Consider the world crucified to you and you to it –

In the book of Galatians, the apostle Paul talks a lot about crucifixion, although his focus is more on how that relates to believers than on the actual act of Jesus being crucified. He says, yes, Jesus was clearly crucified before the world (3:1), but then explains what this means for himself and for all believers in Christ. Paul says believers are also crucified with Christ (2:20). This means that a believer is no longer bound to the passions and desires of their sinful nature (5:24), and it also means the world has been crucified to the believer and the believer to the world (Galatians 6:14).

This is the basis Paul uses when he describes how believers should consider themselves in relation to the world –

- Paul said when we were unbelievers, we lived like everyone else in the world (in disobedience to God), and Satan had us under his power (Ephesians 2:2)

- He said believers died to the world's principles through Christ, so why would we subject ourselves to them anymore (Colossians 2:8)

- Paul said believers should not be conformed to the world any longer (Romans 12:12)

- He said believers are not citizens of the world, we are citizens of heaven (Philippians 3:20), and so we should think about heaven (Colossians 3:2)

- Paul said the world is condemned by the Law of God (Romans 3:19), but believers are not condemned (Romans 8:1)
- He also said God will chasten believers when they become too attached to the world, so they won't be condemned with the world (Warning!) (1 Corinthians 11:32)

Authors of other books in the Bible also recognized that believers are not part of the world –

- The author of Hebrews said of Abraham, that even in the land that God told him to go to, he lived 'as in a foreign country' (11:9)
- He also said in that same chapter, in what is known as the saints' hall of fame, that they all lived as foreigners and strangers on earth (verse 13, NIV), and they all desired to be back in their heavenly country (verses 16)
- The apostle Peter said believers are foreigners and exiles in this world (1 Peter 2:11, NIV)
- He also said believers have spent enough time in the past living like the rest of the world does, and that we should not live like that any longer (1 Peter 4:3)
- The apostle John said the world does not know us, because the world does not know Jesus (1 John 3:1)

Considering oneself a soldier of Christ, and being crucified with Christ to the world, are both good examples from God's Word to help us come out from the world and be separate; but there are more.

Believers should rely on God's grace which teaches us to reject the desires of the world –

The concept of God's grace teaching us to reject the desires of the world (Titus 2:12) involves a few things. First is the fact that we should be extremely thankful that God is gracious and merciful and provided a way for us to be reconciled to Him and not punished eternally for our sins (Romans 7:25, NIV). He didn't have to do that. Second, God did not leave us alone to try to keep our faith in Him, and to follow Him, but He gave us His Holy Spirit to live inside us and to help us do those things (John

Chapter 10: Come Out of the World and Be Separate

14:16, 16:13). He didn't have to do that either. Third, because God can't lie (Titus 1:2), and it is impossible for Him to lie (Hebrews 6:18), we know the promises of our salvation by His saving grace through faith are so certain, that we can reject what the world has to offer, because we know it only leads to death (Proverbs 14:12, Romans 6:23a).

Here are some other things from the Bible that help us to better understand what it means to rely on God's grace and reject the desires of the world –

- Believers have received the Spirit of God, not the spirit of the world (1 Corinthians 2:12)
- The indwelling of the Holy Spirit allows us to share in God's divine nature, which helps us escape the desires of the world (2 Peter 1:4)
- Everyone who is born of God overcomes the world (1 John 5:4)
- As Jesus is, so are believers in this world (1 John 4:17)
- Do not love the world or anything in the world (1 John 2:15)
- Whoever loves their life in this world will lose it (John 12:25)
- Setting your mind on earthly things leads to destruction (Philippians 3:18-19)
- Even believers can love their lives in this world to death (Revelation 12:11)
- Friendship with the world is hatred towards God, and anyone who chooses to be a friend with the world makes themselves an enemy of God (James 4:4). Wow! This is one of the most crystal-clear warnings from the Bible that we must come out of the world and be separate from it. The Greek word for 'hatred' is exthra (ek-thra) and it means the *exact opposite* of agape love. The Greek word for 'enemy' is exthros (ek-thros) and it it the same word used to describe Satan as an enemy of God!
- The world doesn't know Christ, but we know Him, because He lives in us (John 14:17)

Ask God for wisdom to live separate from the world –

According to the world, wisdom is the application of experience and knowledge in order to make good decisions, and technically this is correct. However, God's Word says fear of the Lord is required *to even have wisdom*; and knowledge of the Holy One is required to have understanding (Proverbs 9:10). So, according to God, true wisdom is only possible when a person who fears God applies the experience and knowledge of knowing Him in order to make good decisions.

This is important to understand because God says over and over again in His Word to get wisdom, but now you know He's talking about wisdom that is based in the fear of God and knowledge of the Holy One. With that said, the book of Proverbs is filled with commands for the children of God to seek wisdom (4:5, 7, 7:4, 8:11, 16:16, 19:8, 23:23, 24:3, 14, 29:3); saying wisdom is the most important thing (4:7), and nothing can be compared with the importance of acquiring wisdom (8:11). We are also told that true wisdom comes only from God (Proverbs 2:6), and that if anyone lacks wisdom, to ask God and He will give it to them (James 1:5). What a wonderful invitation and promised blessing for those who truly desire to gain the wisdom that only God can provide.

This wisdom from God will only further help us to live separate from the world by showing us these things from His Word as well –

- Pure religion in the sight of God is caring for those who cannot care for themselves, and also keeping oneself from being corrupted by the world (James 1:27, NLT)

- Live clean, innocent lives as children of God, shining like a bright light in a world full of crooked and perverse people (Philippians 2:15)

- The lust of the flesh, the lust of the eyes and the pride of life are things of this world (John 2:16). Believers should get rid of these, as well as bitterness, rage, anger, foul language, slander and all types of evil behavior (Ephesians 4:31, NLT)

- Believers are to keep themselves free from idols (1 John 5:21)

Chapter 10: Come Out of the World and Be Separate

- Do not associate with anyone who claims to be a believer if they are habitually immoral, greedy or idolaters (1 Corinthians 5:11, NIV)
- Contend for the faith against those in the church who falsely say God's grace makes it ok to live in sin (cheap grace); for those who say and do such things deny Christ (Jude 1:3-4)
- Satan is the god of this world (John 16:11); the whole world is under the power of Satan (1 John 15:19), yet greater is He who is inside a believer (the spirit of God), than he who is in the world (Satan) (1 John 4:4)
- The cares of this world and the deceitfulness of wealth choke the Word of God and make believers unfruitful (Matthew 13:22)
- Worldly Christians do not live by the Spirit, they are infants in Christ (1 Corinthians 3:1), and they need to grow up in their faith (Hebrews 5:12-6:1)
- Believers need to always remember what is seen is temporary, but what is unseen is eternal (2 Corinthians 4:18)

I could go on and on, but will stop here. I pray the Spirit has given you conviction about how important it is for believers in Christ to come out from the world and be separate from it; this is part of our calling. I thank God that Christians who do not come out from the world and live separate from it can still be saved (read the rest of 1 Corinthians 3), but it's clear they won't have anything but the clothes on their backs if they do so. And I'm just guessing (actually I'm not guessing, I'm certain), no one who enters eternity as 'escaping through a wall of flames' (3:15) is going to hear, "Well done, good and faithful servant," when they meet Jesus for the first time.

Well Done, Good and Faithful Servant

Chapter 11

Patiently Endure Suffering

The idea that a Christian must suffer in their walk with Christ their Savior is something that doesn't get a lot of attention, at least not in many of the books that I've read about Christianity; leaving out how Christians must suffer for their faith. Followers of Christ were first called Christians about 42 or 43AD, when the apostle Paul resided for a year in Antioch as a teacher in the church there (Acts 11:26); and many books *have* been written about the sufferings Christians have endured since that time. However, the emphasis tends to focus on *how* they suffered, and not so much that Christians *must* suffer when they follow Christ. This is the case for one simple reason – Jesus was made perfect through His suffering (Hebrews 2:10), and since the process of a believer's sanctification is become more like Him, then Christians should expect to suffer as followers of Christ.

You might say, 'Well, yes, Jesus had to suffer immensely because God the Father poured out His wrath on Jesus for the sins of the world, for yours and mine (Isaiah 53:5), so He had to suffer greatly.' That is correct. However, God's Word also says Jesus learned to be obedient to God the Father through His suffering (Hebrews 5:8-9), and His obedience is what led to His perfection (verse 9). This means that Jesus suffered even before He went to the cross. We see this is true in the Gospels of Matthew 4:1-11, Mark 1:12-13, and Luke 4:1-13, where they all talk about how Satan tempted Jesus, and the Bible confirms He suffered in these temptations (Hebrews 2:18). However, did Jesus really suffer that much when He was tempted by the devil? Yes.

Depending on which account from the Gospels that you read, it says that Jesus was tempted by Satan throughout the entire forty days He was in the desert (Luke 4:2), or He was tempted at the end of those forty days

(Matthew 4:3). Either way, we should not neglect the fact that Jesus fasted during that entire time, because it is in His fasting that we can be sure Jesus suffered while being tempted by the devil (and I'm not talking only about being hungry). Fasting is something believers do to get closer to God. In doing so, they are saying He is more important to them than food; and God will reward His followers when they are fasting in the right way (Matthew 6:17-18).

Now, because fasting is usually done in an attempt to get closer to God, fasting is something believers often do when they really need God's help; when they are calling on Him to step in and do something. It is most likely this is the reason Jesus fasted for forty days, because the temptations of Satan caused Him to suffer greatly, and He wanted to be as close to God the Father as He could to resist those temptations.

Dostoevsky wrote about this in his famous book The Brothers Karamazov. He said, "If there has ever been on earth a real stupendous miracle, it took place on that day, on the day of the three temptations." (1). That's an incredible statement considering all the different kinds of miracles we see in the Bible, including Jesus rising from the dead. Dostoevsky is absolutely amazed that Jesus, being fully human, was still able to resist these temptations of the devil. For what greater desires are there for a human being than to eat, have authority over others, and avoid pain and suffering?

While being tempted, Jesus was extremely hungry, and He absolutely could have turned stones into bread to satisfy His hunger. God can turn stones into people if He wants to (Matthew 3:9). So He could certainly could have turned them into bread; but He didn't. Then Jesus could have shown His authority over the angels by throwing Himself down from the top of the temple and they would not have allowed Him to strike the ground; but He didn't. Lastly, Jesus could have avoided being crucified on a cross as Satan offered to give Him the world (and if the world was His, it would not crucify Him), only if Jesus would bow down and worship him; but He didn't do that either.

Now it's important to note that this world, in its current fallen state, does belong to Satan. We know this is true for a couple reasons. First, when the devil said the world was his and he could give it to anyone he

Chapter 11: Patiently Endure Suffering

wants, Jesus did not say the world was not Satan's. He most certainly would have corrected Satan if that was not the case. Second, God's Word says there will be a time when the world is taken back from the devil and will belong to the Lord again (Revelation 11:15). This means Satan's offer to give Jesus the world so that He would not have to go to the cross was legitimate; and thus, a very real temptation for Jesus that caused Him to suffer in rejecting it.

All this suffering that Jesus did, including going to the cross, He did for you and for me (Galatians 2:20). And because Jesus suffered so much for us when He was here on earth, all believers are called to patiently endure suffering in this world as well. The Bible even says, it is *granted* to believers by God to suffer for Jesus' sake (Philippians 1:29); because Jesus set the example for us (1 Peter 2:20-21).

So, now that we've established that we must suffer as believers because Jesus suffered. How is it that we are supposed to suffer, and how do we learn to suffer patiently? There are three books in the New Testament that teach us ways in which we should expect to suffer, ways in how we should patiently endure suffering, and also ways in which we should not bring unnecessary suffering on ourselves.

In the book of 1st Peter, we see a letter that Peter wrote to 'God's elect' on the subject of suffering as a Christian. The letter was written in the early 60's AD, and the church would have been well established throughout the Roman Empire by this time. The church was beginning to see increased persecution under Emperor Nero, so Peter wrote a letter letting Christians know how they were to patiently endure in their suffering.

Peter said Christians should rejoice in their suffering, because anyone who suffers for being a believer in Christ is proving they have a genuine faith (1 Peter 1:6-7), and their faith will result in the eventual salvation of their souls (verse 9). Peter then calls on them to endure their suffering patiently, which is commendable before God, and to do the same thing Jesus did when He suffered so greatly on the cross – to leave the judgment of those who caused His suffering to the One who judges righteously (2:20-23). He then goes back to exhorting Christians to rejoice in their sufferings that are brought about because of their faith in Christ, and says whoever suffers in such a way is blessed (3:14) because they are taking part in Christ's sufferings (4:13).

Other things Peter says in his letter are that believers should not be surprised when they suffer for Christ (4:12); believers are supposed to suffer, and this is according to the will of God (4:19). However, Peter also says believers should suffer for doing good, not for doing evil (3:17). That no believer should suffer for being a murderer (and remember we can murder someone without actually killing them, see 1 John 3:15), or as a thief, or a gossip, or a doer of any kind of evil (4:15). But rather, since Jesus suffered so much for us in the flesh, that we should have the same mind as Jesus (4:1) and suffer for being a Christian, for this brings glory to God (4:16).

The second letter that has a lot to say about how Christians should patiently endure suffering in this world comes from James, who we already saw was a son of Mary, and brother of Jesus. James eventually became the leader of the church in Jerusalem, and wrote this letter in the mid 40's AD to Jewish believers who were suffering for their faith in Christ.

He begins the letter by saying Christians should consider it a joy to suffer for Christ, since the testing of their faith in this way will produce a patience in them that will, over time, make them perfect and complete in their faith (James 1:2-4). He says when we suffer from temptation, we can be sure the temptations do not come from God, for God does not tempt anyone (1:13). Rather, when we suffer from temptation, it is because we ourselves have moved away from God by our own sinful desires (1:14-15). Like Peter, James exhorts Christians to remove all manner of evil from their lives (1:21), as this will help keep us from suffering things that are not of God's will for us to suffer.

He then goes on to say he sees they are bringing a lot of suffering on themselves through sinful things like lust, murder (through hatred of each other) and covetousness (4:2). That they are asking for things from God out of selfishness, and that their friendship with the world actually is making them out to be adulterers towards God, even His enemies! This is because the Holy Spirit inside believers yearns with a righteous jealousy that we would put God first, and not the things of the world (4:3-5).

Chapter 11: Patiently Endure Suffering

All these sinful things bring unnecessary suffering into our lives, suffering that is not part of God's will. James then tells his listeners how to remove these things from their lives. That they should humble themselves and submit to the Spirit inside them; and to resist the devil. For it is Satan that wishes to keep them apart from God in all these sinful ways (4:7-10).

James then finishes his letter by telling Christians they must patiently endure their sufferings until Jesus returns (or they go to Him) (5:7). He gives the example of a farmer who patiently waits for the crops to grow, and says we should purify our hearts, for the Lord will be coming soon* (5:8). James then says to look upon the example of God's prophets for suffering patiently, and calls them, along with any Christian who patiently endures suffering, as blessed (5:10-11a).

There is a third book in the New Testament that also has a lot to say about suffering as believers in Christ, and that is from an unknown author who wrote the letter of Hebrews. Although the author is unknown, the letter *is* found in God's Word, so we can be sure God intended for it to be there. And we can learn much from this letter to the Hebrews on both how Christians should expect to suffer for God, and how to patiently endure that suffering.

First, we see that Jesus suffered death for us, that He might taste death for everyone (Hebrews 2:9), so that whoever would believe in Him would not perish, but have eternal life (2:10). We read earlier that Jesus was made perfect through His suffering for us (verse 10), and that because of this fact, believers should also expect to suffer towards their perfection (the process of sanctification in the Bible, 1 Thessalonians 4:1-7). But did you know Jesus also had to suffer because He had to experience everything that we experience in order to be our propitiation (substitute) for God's wrath for our sins? (2:17). And this experiencing that Jesus had to do of everything that His brethren (believers) do in their lives, in order to take the wrath of God in their place, would also include their sufferings both physically and mentally.

Jesus certainly experienced our sufferings physically. He knows what it's like to experience pain in a human body, there can be no question about that. However, Jesus also took on our sufferings in ways other than being in physical pain. Jesus knows what it's like to be hungry (Matthew 21:18), He knows what it's like to go without sleep (Luke 6:12), He knows what it's like to become sad to the point of crying (John 11:25), and He knows what it's like to be severely stressed out (Luke 22:44). These are all ways that believers suffer and Jesus had to experience them all, and did.

Now we already learned from the other two books that, in addition to the suffering believers will have to go through because God is going to use it as part of their sanctification process, believers can also bring unnecessary suffering upon themselves because of their sins. The author of the book of Hebrews also talks about this, but he uses a different angle that we must consider as well; that a lot of the suffering we endure as Christians comes from what is called the discipline of God.

The author says since believers struggle against their sinful fleshly desires (and we don't always win those struggles) that God will discipline us in the context of a father disciplining his children when they do wrong (12:4-5, NIV). He adds that God does this out of His love for us (12:6), and that if we are not being disciplined by God then we are not true children of God at all; because all children of God undergo His discipline so that they may become more holy in their behavior (12:7-10, NIV).

So, the book of Hebrews says this is what we can expect from God – His discipline. But what does it say about how are we to endure it? First, the author says we should be more diligent in studying God's Word (2:1), keeping our focus on Jesus and staying faithful to Him (3:1-14); considering that God is always watching His children (4:13). That we should remember Jesus can sympathize with us in our weaknesses because He was tempted in every way that we are; and because of this, we can come to Him and expect to receive His grace, mercy and help (4:15-16).

The book of Hebrews also tells us to strive to grow up in our faith, as this will help us discern between what we should be doing and what we should not be doing (and suffering God's discipline because of it (5:12-14). It says that believers should consider the patience of Abraham. How he patiently endured to the end; and because of his patient endurance he received what was promised him by God (6:13-15). The apostle Paul said this blessing promised to Abraham is also available to all nations through Christ (Galatians 3:14, NIV). Adding that if you are Christ's through faith, you are of Abraham's seed, and thus heirs to the promise God gave to Abraham (Galatians 3:29). So then, since this same promise applies to all believers, it gives us a hope that the author of Hebrews calls an anchor for our souls (6:17-19).

He continues giving advice on how to patiently endure suffering, saying believers should eagerly look for Jesus to return at the Rapture of the church (9:28). But until that time, we should come confidently before the throne of God in prayer because we have been made right with God through the blood of Jesus (10:19). He also says that we should consider one another, to stir up love and good works (10:24), and that believers should not forsake gathering together to support one another (10:25).

The author commends those who joyfully accept their things being taken from them against their will, because one can only do that when they understand they have a better and everlasting possession waiting for them in heaven (10:34). In the same way, he talks of Moses and how he chose to suffer as one of God's people, instead of enjoying the passing pleasures of sin as a son of Pharoah's daughter in a palace. Moses chose suffering because He considered his faith in God of greater riches than all the treasures of Egypt. Looking to the real reward, which is being with God in heaven (11:24-27). Believers would do well to follow these examples.

The book of Hebrews concludes its teachings on patiently enduring suffering by encouraging believers to stay the course, to not grow weary, and to keep our focus on Jesus (12:1-3). The letter also tells us not to despise the discipline of God (12:5); because even though it is not pleasant when we are going through it, over time, God's discipline will produce in His believers a *'harvest of righteousness and peace for those who have been trained by it'* (12:11, NIV).

This can best be compared, I think, to where Jesus describes Himself in the book of John as the true Vine, and God the Father as the Vinedresser (15:1-2). Jesus says believers are the branches coming out of the Vine, and God the Father prunes them so that they may become more fruitful. Pruning involves removal (by cutting off) of diseased, damaged, dead, and otherwise non-productive and unwanted material from the object being pruned. This is done so that it will produce even more fruit than it would have if the unwanted material had been left in place. Now what does that sound like? It sounds just like God's discipline of His believers.

God is cutting off and removing the things in our lives that don't belong there anymore once we come to faith in Christ (Galatians 5:16-21). This act of cutting something off that used to be attached to us will create pain in our lives; but we must endure it patiently, knowing that it is for our own good that God is doing this.

Ultimately, God is doing all this because He wants to give His believers crowns when they get to heaven. These crowns are imperishable (1 Corinthians 9:25), and there are five different kinds – victory (ibid), rejoicing (1 Thessalonians 2:19), righteousness (2 Timothy 4:8), glory (1 Peter 5:4) and life (James 1:12, Revelation 2:10). Now whether these are literal crowns or not isn't the reason I bring them up, but rather to point out that before any crown is awarded there is some form of suffering beforehand that goes along with it.

The victor's crown is associated with running, training and fighting with one's body (against the sinful nature) to make it obedient to God's calling to live a holy life. The crown of rejoicing is associated with the work we do witnessing for Christ, but we suffer for it because Satan is always trying to hinder believers from bringing the Gospel of God's grace to unsaved people. However, we will rejoice greatly when we see those who were saved as a result, when we are all in the presence of Jesus. The crown of righteousness is reserved for those who fight the good fight of witnessing for Jesus in a world that hates Him (this will certainly bring suffering upon those who do so), and also for those who eagerly desire for Jesus to return. How can someone truly desire, even groan in their soul (2 Corinthians 5:2-4), to be with Christ if they are not already suffering in this world?

The apostle Peter talks of a crown of glory for elders in the church. Elders go by many names – pastor, bishop, priest, overseer and others. But the most proper term for them is shepherd. Elders are shepherds for God's people, called by Him to watch over His sheep. The job of a

Chapter 11: Patiently Endure Suffering

shepherd for God's people is not an easy one. Being a servant to God's sheep 24/7 requires a lot of work, and certainly a lot of suffering. Because of this, the Bible says shepherds who do their job well are worthy of a double honor (1 Timothy 5:17); and when the Chief Shepherd appears they will be given a crown of glory that will never perish (1 Peter 5:4).

God's Word says the crown of life will be given to those who love God and to those who faithfully endure temptation (James 1:12). We already saw how temptation produced significant suffering for Jesus, and temptation produces much suffering for believers too. Finally, we see in the last book of the Bible, in Revelation, that Jesus said He will give the crown of life to those who are faithful unto death; and the context is being faithful while suffering for being a follower of Christ. (2:10). So, all five crowns that believers can receive from God are all awarded only after they patiently endure suffering.

Now no discussion about suffering for one's faith in God would be complete without mentioning the quintessential example of suffering in the Bible, found in the book of Job. If ever a person other than Jesus did not deserve to suffer so severely it was Job. He was blameless in his conduct, one who feared God and shunned evil (Job 1:1); and God Himself said there was no one like him in the whole world (1:8).

Satan thought Job would curse God if everything was taken from him, so God allowed it to happen to prove Satan wrong (1:9-12). After Job lost everything, including all ten of his children, Job did not curse God, but rather said, *"The Lord gave, and the Lord has taken away; blessed be the name of the Lord."* (1:21). In the next verse God confirms that, *'In all this Job did not sin nor charge God with wrong.'*

But Satan was not done trying to get Job to curse God. The devil said if Job suffered enough himself, then he would surely curse God. So once again God allowed this to happen to prove Satan wrong (2:4-6), and Job was struck with painful boils from the soles of his feet to the top of his head. Job had three friends who heard what happened to him. They came to see him and sat there with Job, not saying a word for an entire week because they saw how great was his suffering (2:7, 11-13). Even Job's wife told him he should curse God for all that had come upon him, but Job did not curse God. Instead, Job said, *"Shall we indeed accept good from God, and shall we not accept adversity?"* Again, God confirmed that in all this Job did not sin against Him (2:9-10).

Now the story of Job is in the Bible certainly to show that people who follow God are going to suffer, but it is also there to show how believers are to respond to suffering and to endure it patiently. Now anyone who knows the rest of the story knows that Job's 'friends' would go on to not be very good friends at all. Saying he should just admit that he must have brought all this on himself from some kind of sinful behavior that he was not admitting. And Job also does his fair share of complaining that He wants an audience with God to ask why all these things have happened to him; even saying he wished he had never been born (Job 3:3).

However, do not lose sight of the fact that at the end of the story, God says everything Job said about Him was correct (42:7). Including one of the most powerful verses in all of Scripture, in my opinion, where Job gives us this insight in regards to his relationship with God saying, *"Though He slay me, yet will I trust in Him."* (13:15). Ultimately, you cannot trust God any more than that; and anyone that takes that stance will certainly be able to patiently endure suffering until Jesus returns, or they go to meet Him at the death of their body.

Now let's turn to the last step, and it's a big one. Something that will be required for anyone to hear, "Well done, good and faithful servant," when they meet Jesus for the first time; and that is – One must remain faithful until the end.

Chapter 12

One Must Remain Faithful to the End

The idea of once saved always saved is a very controversial topic within the church, but one that needs to be discussed. In the same way that Jesus said he who is not with Me is against Me (Luke 11:23), indicating there is no neutral ground in a person's decision whether Jesus is their Savior or not, there is also no neutral ground on whether a person can lose their salvation or not. Either they can or they cannot. And the implications of whether a person can lose their salvation or not couldn't be more different.

If someone can come to saving faith in Christ, yet somehow lose that salvation later on through verbal denial of Jesus, or a certain level of disobedience that is considered a lack of true saving faith by God, then that person's eternal destination has changed from heaven to hell. If a person comes to saving faith in Jesus, and from that point on, nothing that they say or do can cause them to lose their salvation, then obviously their eternal destination can never change as well. But which one is correct?

If you have read the entire book up to this point (and based on the title of this chapter as well) you know which one I believe is true. I believe God's Word overwhelmingly shows it is possible to go from a state of being saved through faith in Christ, to a state of not being saved through actions that demonstrate there was a change in that person's faith; and it results in God blotting them out of His Book of Life. I know there are far more people in the church that don't believe that than do, but I submit to you that that is one of the reasons why the church is so weak. This is mainly because to believe that once a person has been saved in Christ, if there is nothing that person can say or do to cause them to lose their salvation, this encourages a lack of fear of God.

However, for now, we need to determine which view is correct. Once we do, then we can talk about the ramifications of falling on the wrong side of Scripture in regards to if a person can lose their salvation or not. Since those who believe it is possible for a person to lose their salvation are definitely the minority in the church, I will take the position of the defense and let the once saved always saved proponents have their say first.

I must begin by saying I'm glad that some who preach once saved always saved call those who teach that a person can lose their salvation as preaching a 'harmless heresy.'(1). Since they believe a person cannot lose their salvation, for anyone who believes they can, they say it does no harm to say such things, because it won't change the outcome of either the preacher or the hearers' eternal destination of heaven. So, no harm, no foul. I wish I could call once saved always saved a harmless heresy if it is wrong. But the truth is, if it *is* wrong, then in reality it is anything but harmless. It is a very dangerous heresy.

Are you starting to understand why we need to have this discussion?

So, there are basically three verses in the Bible that once saved always saved proponents focus on to say a person cannot lose their salvation through faith in Christ. There are a few others, but mainly they point to these three verses as quod erat demonstrandum (that is the Latin equivalent of case closed) to try to prove their position of once saved always saved; so we will stick to those three. You will see, however, after scrutinizing just the first two, that it is anything but case closed. From this point on, we will be writing out most of the Scriptures in this chapter, as it is important to let the Holy Spirit do His work within us through the reading of the Word to determine the truth.

The first verse, and probably the one used most often to try to prove once saved always saved, comes from John 10:28-29, *"And I gave them eternal life, and they shall never perish; neither shall anyone snatch them out of My hand. My Father, who has given them to Me, is greater than all; and no one is able to snatch them out of My Father's hand."* This is a wonderful truth from God's Word, and it is true. No one *else* can do anything to affect a person's salvation in Christ; and praise God for that. Because if anyone could, I guarantee you Satan would make sure no one

Chapter 12: One Must Remain Faithful to the End

would be saved. However, the proper context must be considered to see if this truly means there is no way to be removed from Jesus' and the Father's hand once a person comes to saving faith.

If we include the verses before these two, though, it gives the proper context. *"The Jews surrounded Him and said to Him, "How long will you keep us in doubt? If you are the Christ, tell us plainly." Jesus answered them, "I told you, and you do not believe. The works that I do in My Father's name, they bear witness of Me. But you do not believe, because you are not of My sheep, as I said to you. My sheep hear My voice, and I know them, and they follow Me."* (v 24-27). So what does a person have to do to be considered one of Jesus' sheep, and be 'in His hand'? We have to believe that Jesus is the Messiah, the One sent to be our Savior, and we must hear His voice through His Word, and we must follow Jesus.

Does this change once we are considered to be in the hand of Jesus and God the Father? Are these still not conditions that are up to us? Can anyone do anything to change whether we believe, or hear, or follow Jesus? God gives us His Holy Spirit to help us continue to do all those things, but ultimately God's Word says it's up to us to, *"through the power of the Holy Spirit who lives within us, carefully guard the precious truth that has been entrusted to you."* (2 Timothy 1:14).

Does this indicate in any way that the Holy Spirit will *not* allow us to have the choice to not believe, or not to hear, or not to follow Jesus at any point after we come to salvation through faith in Him? If you believe that it does, I have news for you. There is no place for love in that equation. Do you really think God, after someone chooses to freely love Him without the Holy Spirit living inside them, would then make it *impossible* for someone to freely love Him because they have no choice in the matter after the Spirit comes to reside inside them? Is that real love?

So then, if we must be free to choose apart from the Spirit to truly love God, we must also be free to choose whether we believe, or hear, or follow Jesus and God the Father after we are considered to be in their hands. This makes the true context of these verses that no one can snatch us from the hand of Jesus and God the Father – except ourselves. Because we still have the freedom to choose to believe, or not believe, to hear or not to hear, and to follow or not to follow Jesus, even after we come to saving faith in Him.

The second verse that those who believe in once saved always saved bring up often is from 2 Timothy 2:13, *"If we (as believers) are faithless, He (God) remains faithful; He cannot deny Himself."* (Words added for clarification). This is also truth from God's Word; certainly God cannot deny Himself. However, just like with the verses from Matthew, this verse cannot be used apart from the context from which it was given. We need to look at the verses before it and also the context of the entire letter of 2 Timothy. *"For if we died with Him, we shall also live with Him. If we endure, we shall also reign with Him. If we deny Him, He also will deny us."* (2:11-12).

So Paul is first confirming that we're talking about saved believers, those that have died with Christ through faith, and are now alive through the Spirit of God being inside them (Romans 8:9-11). Then he says believers must endure (keep the faith until the end) to reign with Christ, but adds that if we ever deny Him even after the point that we've been saved, Jesus will deny us? Yes. Jesus said exactly this during His ministry on earth. *"Therefore whoever confesses Me before men, him I will also confess before My Father in heaven. But whoever denies Me before men, him I will also deny before My Father in heaven"* (Matthew 10:32-33). If Jesus denies a person before God the Father, are they saved? No.

So is Paul really telling Timothy that if believers are faithless, God remains faithful, and they won't lose their salvation because God cannot deny Himself? He just said in the prior verse that Jesus will deny us if we deny Him. The word Paul uses for 'deny' in the original Greek language in which the New Testament was written is arneomai (ar-neh-om-ahee). It means to disavow, to reject, to renounce. It's the same word that is used where Jesus said if we deny Him, He will deny us (Matthew 10:33). If Jesus disavows, rejects and renounces a person before God the Father, is that person saved? Of course, not.

And don't think this only applies to someone who was never saved through faith in Christ to begin with. To disavow and to renounce means reversing course from the opposite position, which in a believer's case would be one of faith in Christ. So is Paul going to immediately reverse

Chapter 12: One Must Remain Faithful to the End

himself in verse 13 and say if believers later disavow, reject or renounce Jesus that they cannot lose their salvation because God cannot disavow, reject or renounce Himself? Or is it more likely Paul was saying God cannot deny the Holy Spirit that was (past tense) living inside that person, but He *can* deny anyone who disavows, rejects or renounces their faith in Him?

Hopefully you will agree with me that proponents of once saved always saved have tried to take this verse out of context, and it does *not* mean a believer cannot lose their salvation. However, since I'm acting as the defense attorney I'm going to show you there are other examples, both in Paul's first and second letters to Timothy, that show it is not even remotely possible to think Paul was saying believers cannot lose their salvation; because Paul said many things in both letters that indicate believers must remain faithful to the end if they are to be saved.

In Paul's first letter to Timothy (that is preserved as part of God's Word in the Bible) there are no less than nine times where Paul indicates, either through a direct statement, or is implied, that believers must remain faithful to the end or they can lose their salvation that they currently have in Christ.

- *"...love from a pure heart, from a good conscience, and from sincere faith, from which some having strayed have turned aside..."* (1 Timothy 1:6). The word 'strayed' in Greek is astocheo (as-tokh-eh-o) and it means to deviate from truth, to swerve from. Does that sound like someone who still has a true faith in Christ or someone who had it at one time but turned from it?

- *"...having faith and a good conscience, which some having rejected concerning the truth have suffered shipwreck..."* (1 Timothy 1:19). The word 'rejected' in the Greek is apotheomai (ap-o-theh-om-ahee) and it means to cast away or to thrust away from. Paul is saying a person can have saving faith and reject it later. How can someone suffer shipwreck of their saving faith if they never had it to begin with?

- *"He must not be a recent convert, or he may become conceited and fall under the same judgment as the devil."* (1 Timothy 3:6, NIV). The Greek word for 'fall' is empipto (em-pip-to) and it means to fall among. Paul is talking here about bishops and leaders in the church, and says they must not have recently come to saving faith in Christ, otherwise their faith won't be strong enough, and they might *lose their salvation* and end up in the lake of fire with the devil.

- *"Now the Spirit expressly says that in latter times some will depart from the faith..."* (1 Timothy 4:1). The Greek word for 'depart' is aphistemi (af-is-tay-mee) and it means to revolt or desert. Is a person who revolts from saving faith in Christ going to be saved if they remain in that condition until death, or if Jesus comes for the Rapture of the church?

- *"Watch your life and doctrine closely. Persevere in them, because if you do, you will save both yourself and your hearers."* (1 Timothy 4:16, NIV). The Greek word for 'persevere' is epimeno (ep-ee-men-o) and it means to continue in or abide in. That is pretty self-explanatory, we must abide in our faith until the end for it to result in our salvation.

- *"If anyone does not provide for his own, and especially for those of his household, he has denied the faith and is worse than an unbeliever."* (1 Timothy 5:8). The Greek work for 'denied' is the one we already saw in Paul's second letter to Timothy, arneomai, where he said if we deny Jesus then He will deny us. The word means to disavow, to reject, to renounce. I ask again, if a person disavows, rejects and renounces their faith in Christ is that person saved? However, don't miss the fact that Paul is saying a person can disavow, reject and renounce their faith through their actions. This is because persistent, willful disobedience to God will be considered unbelief by Him (Hebrews 4:1-13). And what's more, Paul says someone who once had saving faith, and later loses it, is in a worse condition (worse than an unbeliever) than if they had never been a believer in the first place. Peter says the same thing

Chapter 12: One Must Remain Faithful to the End

in one of his letters too (2 Peter 2:20). How can this happen if it is not possible to go from a state of salvation through faith to one of not being saved? But Paul is saying it *can* happen.

- *"But refuse the younger widows, for when they have begun to grow wanton against Christ, they desire to marry, having condemnation because they have cast off their first faith."* (1 Timothy 5:11-12). There are two phrases here, grow wanton and cast off. The Greek word for grow wanton, and it is only one word but oh what a word it is, is katastreniao (kat-as-tray-nee-ah-o) and it means to become voluptuously undisciplined against, which in this case is against Christ. The Greek word for 'cast off' is atheteo (ath-et-eh-o) which means to disesteem, to consider something as of no value anymore, to act towards something as though it were annulled. That sounds like someone who once had saving faith, but then through their disobedience lost it; and as a result, lost their salvation in Christ. Paul confirms as much a few verses before where he says widows that live for pleasure are 'dead while they live' (5:6). People who are dead while they live are not in a state of salvation in Christ.

- *"For the love of money is a root of all kinds of evil, for which some have strayed from the faith in their greediness..."* (1Timothy 6:10). The Greek word for 'strayed' is apoplanao (ap-op-lan-ah-o) and it means to wander away from the truth. If someone wanders away from the truth of salvation by faith, and they stay there until they die, do you think that person will be saved? And the Bible says greedy people will not inherit the kingdom of God (1 Corinthians 6:10, NIV). So, will a person who was once saved, who wanders away from the truth of salvation through faith, because of their greed for money, still be saved? God's Word says they will not. (Which is all the more reason to give generously, to prove to God you are not greedy for money.)

- *"Turn away from godless chatter and the opposing ideas of what is falsely called knowledge, which some have professed and in doing so have departed from the faith."* (1 Timothy 6:20-21,

NIV). The Greek word for 'departed' is the one that Paul used at the beginning of this letter where he said some have strayed from a sincere faith, astocheo, meaning to deviate from, or swerve from the truth.

Considering all these examples from Paul's first letter to Timothy, do you think it is even *remotely* possible that in Paul's second letter to Timothy in chapter 2, verse 12, that he would have meant once a person comes to saving faith in Christ, that they can never lose that salvation as once saved always saved proponents interpret it? I could stop there in proving that it does not, but I'm going to keep going because we haven't looked at the evidence from Paul's second letter to Timothy. And Paul even gives examples in that letter of people who have gone from a state of salvation in Christ, to one of being unsaved.

First, Paul continues using the same words (and a new one) in the second letter that we saw from the first that indicates a person can lose their salvation in Christ. We see an example where Paul uses the word 'astocheo' to describe two individuals who have deviated and swerved from the truth, and 'anatrepo' (an-at-rep-o) to describe believers that have had their faith destroyed by believing their false doctrine. *"Hymenaeus and Philetus are of this sort, who have astocheo concerning the truth, saying the resurrection is already past, and they anatrepo the faith of some."* (verses 17b-18).

Hymenaeus was mentioned in Paul's first letter to Timothy as one who has rejected the true faith and suffered shipwreck as a result (1:20). We do not see Philetus' name anywhere else in the Bible, but if he is mentioned together with Hymenaeus, we can be sure at one point he had saving faith in Christ and later lost it by teaching false doctrine *that caused others to end up in hell.*

Paul also writes of other people who once had saving faith in Christ but lost it for one reason or another. He says Demas, the same person who was confirmed in the Bible as being a true believer in Christ two times (Colossians 4:14. Philemon 1:24), has now deserted Paul (and most certainly his saving faith) for the pleasures of this world (2 Timothy 4:10). Paul also tells of a man named Alexander who did a lot of harm to him. He also was once a true believer in Christ, but suffered shipwreck of his

Chapter 12: One Must Remain Faithful to the End

faith as well (1 Timothy 1:20), and now greatly resists Paul's teachings of the true gospel (2 Timothy 4:14). Do you really believe Alexander was still saved in Christ simply because he was at one time before? Paul asked God be his avenger on Alexander (ibid). Do believers ask God to punish other believers in hell, for all eternity? God's Word says if they do that, they are in danger of going to hell themselves! (Matthew 5:22, any version of the Bible, but best described in the NASB).

If Paul had even given *one* example of a person that was once saved through their faith in Christ, but lost it later, that should be enough; but we've already seen at least four. So we can be sure that Paul, in no way whatsoever, teaches once saved always saved in any of his letters in the Bible.

In keeping with those same examples of people in the Bible who were once saved through faith in Christ but then lost their salvation, what about Judas who was an apostle of Christ? God's Word says Judas was, at least for a time, an apostle of Jesus (Matthew 10:2-4, Luke 6:13-16). Can one be an apostle of Jesus yet not be saved while they are considered to be an apostle? Paul said apostles are at the top of the appointments of God in the church (1 Corinthians 12:28); and Paul said of himself that he was an apostle (1 Corinthians 9:1). Could it be that Paul, the greatest evangelist in the history of mankind, could still lose his salvation if he wasn't faithful until the end? Yes. Paul himself said if he wasn't careful in controlling his sinful desires, he could lose his salvation (1 Corinthians 9:24-10:15).

There are many who say, including those who preach once saved always saved, that Judas never had saving faith in Christ. But they *must* teach that in order for their doctrine to hold water. In reality, God's Word says Judas had saving faith for a time, but then lost it when he betrayed Jesus. Believers would be wise to consider Judas as the penultimate example of how someone could be that close to Jesus for three years, and have saving faith during much of that time, yet then lose it through a loss of faith that was displayed through his betrayal. And if one even wants to try to say, 'Well, then maybe Judas did have saving faith, and because he did, he must have been saved despite his betrayal.' To that I would say, the Bible confirms from both Peter (Acts 1:17-18) and Jesus Himself (John 17:12), that Judas lost his salvation and went to hell as a result.

The third verse that once saved always saved teachers bring up again and again is from Hebrews, chapter 13, verse 5. *"For He Himself has said, "I will never desert you, nor will I ever abandon you."* (NASB). This time I even chose the version that seems to offer the strongest argument for their case. However, once again, they are trying to take a verse and make it stand alone without interpreting the Scripture with the verses around it; nor considering the dozens of other verses throughout the entire Bible that say otherwise.

In this case though, we don't even have to use any other verses, we just need to include the rest of *that* verse to see the context is wrong. The entire verse reads, *"Make sure that your character is free from the love of money, being content with what you have; for He Himself has said, "I will never desert you, nor will I ever abandon you."* The context is money, and that a believer should be content with what God has given them; because God will always take care of those who look to Him for their needs. The second part of this verse cannot just be cut off and used as an example to teach once saved always saved without any regard to the context, or consideration for the dozens of examples in the Bible that say otherwise. That is not rightly dividing the Word of God, as teachers are told they must be able to do (2 Timothy 2:15).

I find it very ironic that one of the three verses that once saved always saved proponents point to again and again comes from a letter whose entire purpose was to tell a group of believers that if they abandon their faith in Christ, they will end up losing the salvation that they currently possess; and will end up in hell if they die in that condition. I mentioned in the introduction that there are two entire books in God's Word devoted to teaching a group of believers that they had better not renounce their faith in Christ (verbally or through their actions) or they would fall from God's saving grace and lose their salvation – Galatians and Hebrews. Since we already looked at a verse from Hebrews, let's start there.

In some of the other steps in this book, we have already seen many quotes from God's Word from the book of Hebrews. Most recently where we looked at the many examples it gives on how to patiently endure suffering. The author of the book also gives many examples concerning how one must remain faithful to the end to be saved. In fact, this is the

Chapter 12: One Must Remain Faithful to the End

very purpose for which the book was written. The book of Hebrews was written in the early 60's AD to a group of Jewish believers who were being persecuted so severely for their faith that they were considering going back to Judaism.

It is because of this persecution that we find so many ways in the book on how to patiently endure it. However, because the book was written primarily to show them Jesus is the Christ (the Messiah) and to turn away from their newfound faith in Him would result in them losing their salvation, we also find many statements in Hebrews that a person can be saved in Christ, but then lose that salvation if they do not remain faithful to the end. In addition to some of the Greek words we have already seen from Paul that shed more light on what he was trying to say, we see other words in the book of Hebrews that have not been presented yet. So let's do the same exercise that proved so effective in better understanding Paul's letters to Timothy, and show how the original Greek makes the author's statements that much more clear to us.

- *"We must pay the most careful attention, therefore, to what we have heard, so that we do not drift away. For since the message spoken through angels was binding, and every violation and disobedience received its just punishment, how shall we escape if we ignore so great a salvation?"* (2:1-3a, NIV). The Greek for 'drift away' is pararrhueo (par-ar-hroo-eh-o) and it means to carelessly pass by without giving heed to something that deserves attention. Wow, what a word. There is no translation in English but the message is clear. No one will escape condemnation for their sins if they don't take seriously God's only method of salvation through a true faith in Jesus Christ.

- *"For every house is built by someone, but He who built all things is God...but Christ as a Son over His own house, whose house we are if we hold fast the confidence and the rejoicing of the hope firm to the end."* (2:4, 6). The Greek for 'hold fast' is katecho (kat-ekh-o) and it means to hold down to prevent the progress of something. Prevent the progress of what? In the context of the verse before it, to prevent the progress of losing one's faith before the end; because if we do, we are no longer part of the house of Christ, His church.

- *"Beware brethren, lest there be in any of you an evil heart of unbelief in departing from the living God...For we have become partakers of Christ, if we hold the beginning of our confidence steadfast to the end."* (3:12, 14). The word for 'departing' in Greek is one we've seen before from Paul's letters to Timothy, aphistemi. It means to revolt or to desert. The word for 'hold' is the same as we saw in the last example for hold fast, katecho. This is one of the most clear, irrefutable warnings from God's Word that a person can lose their salvation in Christ. He begins 'beware brethren,' so is he considering them saved at this point? Yes. Then he says, but if you depart from God - and Jesus even used this same word aphistemi, in Luke 8:13, to say believers *can* revolt and desert Him - then you will lose your salvation.

- *"Let us therefore be diligent to enter that rest, lest anyone fall according to the same example of disobedience."* (4:11). The Greek word for 'fall' is pipto (pip-to) and it means to fall down from. Fall down from what? The author just spent the last 13 verses before this explaining how the Israelites did not get to enter into the land that God wanted to give them because of their disobedience in following Him. He then added that believers in his day (and ours too, this is not just for Jewish believers) can also lose the blessings God wants to give them through their disobedience to Him. Except in their case and ours, it doesn't mean a loss of land, it means a loss of eternal salvation!

- *"Therefore since we have a great High Priest who has ascended into heaven, Jesus the Son of God, let us hold firmly to the faith that we profess."* (4:14, NIV). The Greek for 'hold firmly' is krateo (krat-eh-o) which means to take hold of with strength. Believers must hold onto their faith, because there are others (Satan and his fallen angels) and other things (the world and even our own culture) that are trying to destroy it. Satan knows, he absolutely knows, that if he can destroy a person's faith it will result in them going to hell instead of heaven. Why else would God's Word describe him as a roaring lion looking for a believer to devour? (1 Peter 5:8).

- *"For it is impossible for those who were once enlightened, and have tasted the heavenly gift, and have become partakers of the Holy Spirit, and have tasted the good Word of God and the powers of the age to come, if they fall away, to renew them again to repentance, since they crucify again for themselves the Son of God, and put Him to an open shame."* (6:4-6). The Greek word for 'fall away' is parapipto (par-ap-ip-to) which is a version of a word we already saw, pipto. Para means 'by,' so parapipto means to fall down by. In this case, it would mean to fall down by a lack of repentance and faith.

This is also a very strong warning that a believer can lose their salvation due to a lack of faith or disobedience, because the verse confirms he's talking about believers; those who have the Spirit of God living inside them. And if they fall away after they profess to be believers in Christ, then they bring shame to the One who died for them. I think this verse is referring to cheap grace.

Anyone who thinks they can profess to be saved through the blood of Christ, yet live in a way that indulges the sinful nature definitely brings shame to Jesus and treats as a mockery what He endured on the cross. God's Word has a very stern warning for people like that, and it comes from (surprise) the book of Hebrews – *"How much more severely do you think someone deserves to be punished who has trampled the Son of God underfoot, who has treated as an unholy thing the blood of the covenant that sanctified them (this applies to believers only), and who has insulted the Spirit of grace? For we know Him who said, "It is mine to avenge; I will repay," and again, The Lord will judge His people." It is a dreadful thing to fall into the hands of the living God."* (Hebrews 10:29-31, NIV, words in parenthesis added for clarification).

- *"Therefore do not cast away your confidence (faith), which has great reward."* (10:35, word added in parenthesis for clarification). The Greek word for 'cast away' is apoballo (ap-ob-al-lo) and it means to throw off from. Knowing the definition of the original language in which it was written, is there any way to translate this other than it *is* possible for believers to separate themselves from the saving faith that they once had? This would, of course, mean they would not be in a position of salvation through faith in Christ anymore either.

- *"Now the just shall live by faith; But if anyone draws back, My soul has no pleasure in him. But we are not of those that draw back to perdition, but of those who believe to the saving of the soul."* (10:38-39). The Greek word for 'draw back' is hupostello (hoop-os-tel-lo) and it means to withdraw from. Withdraw from what? From their faith. And the author says it is possible to withdraw from one's faith to the point of perdition (no salvation). We can be certain that's what he means, because he says the opposite of that is to believe to the saving of the soul.

The book of Hebrews offers one of the best defenses in the New Testament of why Jesus is the Messiah spoken of in the Old Testament, and it spends many chapters proving it. However, that is not the main reason the book is there. Think about it. If once saved always saved was true, it shouldn't matter if Jewish believers (or any believers for that matter), after coming to a genuine saving faith in Christ, would leave that faith later in life. But we can see from the examples given, the author of Hebrews doesn't believe there is such a thing as once saved always saved. He wrote the letter precisely because he *knew* there wasn't, and if those believers for whom the letter was intended did go back to Judaism, they would, in fact, lose their salvation in Christ.

So now we've seen leaving one's faith in Christ can cause a person to lose their salvation, but what about those who want to add works to their faith, as if there is anything they can do to help earn their salvation? This was addressed in the other book in the Bible written for the purpose of showing a group of believers (and us too) that they had better be careful,

Chapter 12: One Must Remain Faithful to the End

because if they thought they had to add a list of requirements other than faith alone to be saved, they could also lose their salvation. This is why the book of Galatians was written.

The author is the apostle Paul, and it is the first letter he wrote that is preserved forever as a part of God's Word (1 Peter 1:23-25, 2 Peter 3:16). It was written about 49AD, and we can be sure of that because he mentions in the letter a recent council in Jerusalem that took place in that same year (Galatians 2:1-5). Paul was writing to the churches in Galatia which he had established a few years earlier during his first missionary journey to that region. He wrote the letter in response to rumors that the churches there were practicing Judaism in addition to trying to follow Christ.

Paul begins in the harshest of terms to tell them that is not something that can save them –

"I am astonished that you are so quickly deserting the One who called you to live in the grace of Christ and are turning to a different gospel – which is really no gospel at all. Evidently some people are throwing you into confusion and are trying to pervert the gospel of Christ." (1:6-7, NIV)

The English translation is pretty self-explanatory, one cannot desert the true gospel of God's saving grace through faith in Christ and expect to be saved by it, but let's look at two Greek words to solidify this understanding. The Greek word for 'desert' is metatithemi (met-at-ith-ay-mee) and it means to transfer or change sides. The Greek word for 'pervert' is metastrepho (met-as-tref-o) and it means to transform into something else. If a believer changes sides and follows a gospel that has been transformed into something other than the true gospel of Christ can they expect to be saved by it?

Paul calls the ones he is talking to in the letter his brethren (1:11), so he considers them people who are (or were at one time anyway) believers in the true gospel; and saved. But what were they doing that threatened their salvation in Christ? They were trying to follow the laws found in Judaism in addition to following Christ, and Paul says they cannot do that–

> *"O foolish Galatians! Who has bewitched you that you should not obey the truth, before whose eyes Jesus Christ was clearly portrayed among you as crucified? This only I want to learn from you: Did you receive the Spirit by the works of the law, or by the hearing of faith? Are you so foolish? Having begun in the Spirit, are you now being made perfect by the flesh?" (3:1-3)*

Paul says in the next verse to live in this way will cause one to lose their salvation, "Have you suffered so many things in vain?" This could only mean their suffering for following Christ would not result in their salvation if they continued to live in this way. Paul said the law is not of faith (3:12), and the purpose of the law is to lead us to Christ, that we might be saved by faith (3:24), and not by continuing to try to earn our way into heaven (4:9-10). Paul said because they were living like this, he was concerned whether or not they were still saved by faith (4:11).

Does it sound like Paul believes in once saved always saved? And if everything we already saw from his letters to Timothy, and now from Galatians, isn't proof enough, Paul says plainly to the believers in Galatia that if they think something like circumcision is necessary to be saved, then they have definitely lost their salvation in Christ –

> *"Indeed I, Paul, say to you that if you become circumcised, Christ will profit you nothing... You have become estranged from Christ, you who attempt to be justified by the law; you have fallen from grace." (5:2, 4)*

We don't have to look at any Greek words to understand what this says, but we're going to do it anyway. The Greek word for 'profit' is opheleo (o-fel-eh-o) and it means to be useful to. The Greek word for 'estranged' is katargeo (kat-arg-eh-o) and it means to reduce to zero. The Greek word for 'fallen' is ekpipto (ek-pip-to) and it means to be driven out.

So, what Paul said here in his summation of his letter to the Galatians was if you think you can be saved by anything that you do, other than simply through faith in the One that already did everything for you, Christ will not be useful to you at all. You have become completely cut off from Him (zero benefit), and as a result, have been driven out from His saving

Chapter 12: One Must Remain Faithful to the End

grace. Does that sound like a person who is still saved in Christ? No, of course not.

There are at least two other examples in the Bible that talk about being cut off from Christ. One comes also from Paul in his letter to the believers in Rome. In chapter 11, he compares Jewish believers to being branches in the tree of Abraham, and says that because the root and tree are holy, so are the branches (verse 16). He then says some of the Jewish branches have been broken off because of unbelief. And that any non-Jewish (Gentile) believer becomes grafted into the tree of Abraham and of Israel when they come to saving faith in Christ (even though they are considered to be from a different kind of tree, verses 17-18). We already talked about this, how non-Jewish believers can share in the promises of Abraham, and this is another example confirming it.

Paul then says, however, that we should not boast against the other natural branches (which is a warning to anyone who says God has rejected Israel, He has not (Jeremiah 31:35-37), and that non-Jewish believers should fear God, because if He did not spare the natural Jewish branches and severed them off the tree because of unbelief, He will certainly not spare Gentile believers who lose their faith as well (v 20-21). Does this analogy in any way illustrate that a believer, especially a non-Jewish believer, once they have been grafted into Christ through faith, cannot then be severed from Christ if they revert back to a state of unbelief? It doesn't say that at all, it says the exact opposite.

And what of Christ Himself? What did Jesus say about the possibility of being a branch that can be severed from Him; and what would happen to the branches that were broken off? Jesus said He is the Vine, and branches that were connected to him (people who were in Christ, saved), that if they did not produce any fruit, they would be severed; cut off from Him (John 15:1-2). And where does God's Word say branches that are severed from Christ go if they die in that state of being cut off in unbelief? They get thrown into the fire in hell (verse 6).

In the last book of the Bible, Revelation, we find seven letters to the churches written by the apostle John, and narrated to him by Jesus. Here we see more confirmation directly from Jesus that believers must remain faithful to the end if they are to be saved. Jesus says believers must be faithful unto death to receive the crown of life (2:10), and that believers must hold fast to what they have (their salvation through faith) so that no one will take their crown of life from them (3:11). For those that do remain faithful to the end, Jesus says He will not blot their name out of the Book of Life; and He will confess that person's name before God the Father (3:5). For Jesus to say He will not blot someone's name out of the Book of Life shows that it is certainly possible for the opposite to happen, *to be blotted out* of the Book of Life.

It was my intention when I began writing this chapter to show you every single reference that I could find in God's Word that indicates a person can go from being saved through a faith in Christ, to not being saved; either by losing their faith or God considering their faith dead through their disobedience. And if I were to do that at this point, it would require at least ten more pages even if we covered each verse with only the briefest of commentary.

I think, however, it would be best to put those references into an appendix for those who choose to read them, and stop here. I'm very well aware that the majority of people who have read this chapter, especially if you skipped to the end to read it, probably believed there was nothing you could do to lose your salvation in Christ, but now see that is not the case; and I'm sure you have been rocked to the core. I understand. It's scary to know that it is our responsibility to remain faithful to the end if we are to receive eternal life in Christ. There are so many things in this world (including our own sinful nature) that are trying to pull us away from God and His grace.

And to tell you the truth, I do wish it was the other way around. That once I came to saving faith in Christ, that there was no way that I could possibly lose that salvation. But think about it for a minute. If God is going to prepare a place for believers that is so wonderful that no eye has seen, no ear has heard, no mind has conceived how truly incredible that place is (1 Corinthians 2:9), don't you think that would be something that God would want you to have the choice to be a part of or not? And don't forget the biggest part of all that 'wonderfulness' is going to be worshipping and fellowshipping with God the Father and Jesus in their presence.

Chapter 12: One Must Remain Faithful to the End

If once we come to saving faith in Christ, however, if God no longer allows us the ability to change our mind, or the possibility of being pulled away from Him by the world, is our faith in Him really real at that point? An honest answer is no, it would not be a genuine faith if it was out of our control and not our responsibility to stay faithful.

So where does that leave us? If you are a child of God through faith in Christ, I'd say that means you are in a pretty good place. For the Lord knows how to rescue His children from a world that He has reserved for punishment (2 Peter 2:9). Cling to Him with all your might, and make your number one goal to try to hear, "Well done, good and faithful servant," when you meet the Lord Jesus for the first time, and you will be fine.

Maranatha!

Well Done, Good and Faithful Servant

Appendix

When I began writing the last chapter of the book, it was my full intention to list every verse that I could find from the Bible that seems to prove without a doubt that a person *can* in fact go from being saved through faith in Christ, to not being saved; either from rejecting that faith later on, or through persistent willful disobedience that God would consider a lack of saving faith.

However, after going through a little more than half of the sixty or so passages from Scripture that I had prepared to use in defense, it became overwhelming evident that once saved always saved proponents don't have much to stand on compared to the mountain of evidence from God's Word that says otherwise. And to continue listing every passage seemed to be getting to the point where I might be going against God's commands to love my brothers and sisters. Because rather than gently trying to help them see that according to God's Word once saved always saved is wrong, to continue to list verse after verse might look more like I was throwing God's Word in their face, and that is not my intention. I simply want the truth of God's Word to speak to each and every reader of this book so they can understand that they *must remain faithful to the end* (until they die or Jesus returns at the Rapture) if they want to be saved.

So, for that reason, I felt compelled to stop when I believed the evidence from God's Word could not be denied that a believer *can* lose their salvation if they are not faithful until the end. However, since I did say at the start of the book that I was going to show you over fifty verses in defense, and because I know there are still people reading this book that *do* want to see all of them, here are many more along with some commentary on each.

> *"Then Moses returned to the Lord and said, "Oh these people have committed a great sin, and have made for themselves a god of gold! Yet now, if You will forgive their sin – but it not, I pray, blot me out of Your Book which You have written." And the Lord said to Moses, "Whoever has sinned against Me, I will blot him out of My Book." – Exodus 32:31-33*

God's Book of Eternal Life is mentioned in both the Old and New Testaments. You *must* have your name in the Book of Life in order to inherit eternal life. And you can see, both here in the Old Testament and in the New Testament (Revelation 3:5), God says He will blot out the names of people who were in the Book (saved until that moment) that were not faithful to the end. If a person is blotted out of God's Book of Life, are they still saved?

> *And the Lord said to Moses: "Behold, you will rest with your fathers, and this people will rise and play the harlot with the gods of the foreigners of the land, where they go to be among them, and they will forsake Me and break My covenant which I have made with them. Then My anger shall be aroused against them in that day, and I will forsake them, and I will hide My face from them, and they shall be devoured." – Deuteronomy 31:16-17a*

I included this verse because it also refutes one of the three passages that once saved always saved proponents use again and again from Hebrews 13:5, *"For He Himself has said, "I will never leave you nor forsake you."* The first time I brought up this verse I used the NASB version which uses 'abandon' instead of 'forsake.' So now let's use the word that is cited more often from the NIV version, forsake. We see from Deuteronomy that God *will* forsake those who don't remain faithful to Him. And like I said before, that verse is being taken completely out of context, because when including the first twelve chapters of Hebrews before that verse, it should be obvious what the author is saying is *if we stay faithful to God*, He will never leave us or forsake us.

> *"Now the Spirit of God came upon Azariah the son of Obed. And he went out to meet Asa, and said to him: "Hear me Asa, and all Judah and Benjamin. The Lord is with you while you are with Him. If you seek Him, He will be found by you; but if you forsake Him, He will forsake you." – 2 Chronicles 15:2*

Just in case anyone still thinks the Lord God (who is our Savior Jesus) will not forsake a believer who first forsakes Him; how much more proof do you need? The key is, *if we remain faithful*, He will never leave us, nor forsake us. That is a wonderful promise from God. But if we forsake

Him first, and die without coming back to the Lord through faith, even if we *were* saved at one time, we will lose our salvation.

> *"I greatly regret that I have set up Saul as king, for he has turned back from following Me, and has not performed My commandments." 1 Samuel 15:11*

> *"But the Spirit of the Lord departed from Saul, and a distressing spirit from the Lord troubled him." – 1 Samuel 16:14*

Even in the Old Testament we see God does not force people to follow Him. Saul turned from following the Lord, *it was Saul's choice*; and the Spirit of the Lord, the same Spirit that gives life and salvation when He resides inside us, left Saul after he turned away from the Lord.

> *" I (the Lord) gave faithless Israel her certificate of divorce and sent her away because of all her adulteries." – Jeremiah 3:8, NIV (words in parenthesis added for clarification)*

To get a certificate of divorce means the two involved must first be married. The Lord God and Israel were married, but He divorced them because their persistent, willful disobedience was viewed by the Lord as a lack of faith (faithless). Remember, believers are already married to Jesus, just like Israel was, so don't think He cannot give a believer today a certificate of divorce if they are found to be faithless through disobedience.

> *"Your wickedness will bring its own punishment. Your turning from Me will shame you. You will see what an evil, bitter thing it is to abandon the Lord your God and not to fear Him." – Jeremiah 2:19, NLT*

Here again we see that God does not force people to follow Him. He doesn't force us to come to saving faith in Him, and He doesn't force us to stay in that faith. This passage also says a person can turn from Him, and abandon Him. To turn from and abandon someone means, at one point, you had to be 'with them.' Is someone who turns from and abandons the Lord God still saved?

> *"When I tell righteous people that they will live, but then they sin, expecting their past righteousness to save them, then none of their righteous acts will be remembered. I will destroy them for their sins...For again I say, when righteous people turn away from their righteous behavior and turn to evil, they will die."* – Ezekiel 33:13, 18, NLT

The only way to be considered righteous before the Lord is through faith. So if God declares someone righteous through faith, yet they turn away from that faith through persistent sinful, evil behavior, the fact that they were saved at one time will not help them; because God says those who turn from their faith *will not* inherit eternal life.

> *"For if you forgive other people when they sin again you, your heavenly Father will also forgive you. But if you do not forgive others their sins, your Father will not forgive your sins."* – Matthew 6:14-15, NIV

Believers must forgive others, because Jesus first has forgiven them (Colossians 3:13). God is very serious about this. Jesus illustrated this in the parable of the unmerciful servant. The servant was forgiven a debt by his master that was impossible to pay back (two hundred thousand years' worth of wages), yet that servant then went out and did not forgive someone who owed him absolutely nothing in comparison (one day's wage). When the master found out what happened, he called that servant 'wicked,' reinstated the impossible amount of debt, and handed him over to be tortured until it was paid back. Of course, it could not be paid back, so that former servant would be tortured forever.

The analogy is the debt we owe to God for what He did for us in dying on the cross for our sins, and rising again from the dead for our eternal life is impossible for us to repay. And if God is going to forgive us a debt that would take two hundred thousand years to pay off, yet we will not forgive someone who owes us only one day's wage, then God will remove us from His Book of Life, reinstate our debt that cannot be repaid, and torture us in hell for all eternity. This parable does not apply to non-believers, it applies to believers; someone who was already forgiven their

Appendix

two hundred thousand years' worth of debt, but you can see it can be reinstated (loss of salvation) if we do not forgive others.

> *"And you will be hated by all for My name's sake. But he who endures to the end will be saved." – Matthew 10:22*

The Greek word for 'endures' is hupomeno (hoop-om-en-o), and it means to abide under. So, this is saying believers must abide under Jesus (through faith) to the end to be saved. Why would Jesus say this if it was not possible for someone to *not* abide under Him once that person becomes saved through faith?

> *"A certain man had a fig tree planted in his vineyard, and he came seeking fruit on it and found none. Then he said to the keeper of his vineyard, 'Look, for three years I have come seeking fruit on this fig tree and find none. Cut it down; why does it use up the ground? But he answered him and said to him, 'Sir, let it alone this year also, until I dig around it and fertilize it. And if it bears fruit, well. But if not, after that you can cut it down." – Luke 13:6-9*

We've seen this type of parable before with Jesus as the Vine and God the Father as the Vinedresser. In this case, the certain man is Jesus and the keeper of His vineyard is God the Father. This parable is actually talking about the nation of Israel*, and how Jesus would minister to them for three years before the leaders of Israel would put Jesus to death, and how God the Father would end up cutting down the 'fig tree' of Israel (and did in 70AD).

That being said, this is still an example of someone, a nation this time, going from being in Jesus' vineyard (saved), to being cut down (not saved); and this is a warning for America as well. If God did not spare Israel when they stopped producing fruit, He will not spare the one other nation that absolutely was the result of His doing to produce 'fruit' for the world, which was America. Do you realize where this world would be without America to keep the peace and help those in need? America was definitely an instrument of God to keep the world from collapsing before the appointed time. Nevertheless, once America stops producing fruit (and I would say that day is fast approaching), God will not spare America either.

> *"Salt is good for seasoning. But if it loses its flavor, how do you make it salty again? Flavorless salt is good neither for the soil nor for the manure pile. It is thrown away. Anyone with ears to hear should listen and understand." – Luke 14:34-35, NLT*

Jesus compared believers in Him to salt (Matthew 5:13), so He's talking about believers here. If a believer loses their flavor (their faith that makes them 'salt') they aren't fit for use for anything in the kingdom of God, and are thrown away (lose their salvation).

> *"Which man of you, having a hundred sheep, if he loses one of them, does not leave the ninety-nine in the wilderness and go after the one which is lost until he finds it? ...And when he comes home, he calls together his friends and neighbors, saying to them, 'Rejoice with me, for I have found my sheep which was lost!' I say to you likewise that there will be more joy in heaven over one sinner who repents than over ninety-nine just persons who need no repentance." – Luke 15:4-7*

Almost everyone has heard this parable before, but have you considered that the lost sheep was a person who was once saved (one of Jesus' sheep), but then was 'lost' again (unsaved)? The context is the sheep became lost when it stopped repenting of its sins. This is a form of cheap grace. If a believer thinks they can use God's grace to go on sinning without repentance, God will consider them 'lost,' which means not saved.

The next example is of the prodigal son, also from Luke chapter 15; and rather than write it out (because it is a long parable), I will summarize. The parable talks of a son who asks his father for his share of the inheritance before the father dies. This is the same as saying, 'Father, I wish you were dead so that I can have my share of the inheritance.' To the surprise of the hearers then (and now) the father agrees to give his son his share of the inheritance. This could not happen unless the son was a believer, as non- believers do not have any inheritance from God the Father (Matthew 25:31-46).

Appendix

When the son leaves, it is likened to one turning from God and losing his salvation. How do we know this? Because the parable says when the son came to his senses, he repented of his sin (15:17-19), and the father forgave him (verses 20-24). That sounds good, but how do we know the son went from a state of salvation, to not being saved, to saved again? The key is in verse 24 where the father said, *"This son of mine was dead and is alive again; he was lost and is found."* The key is the word 'again,' the father said his son was alive *again*. So his son went from someone who was part of the father's household (saved) to receive his inheritance, to someone who wasn't saved when he left the father's household (of his own doing I might add), to someone who was saved *again*. How can it not be any clearer than that? That a believer can go from saved, to not saved, to saved again (and praise God we can be saved again if we lose our salvation for a time).

> *"And the Lord said, "Simon, Simon! Indeed, Satan has asked for you, that he may sift you as wheat. But I have prayed for you, that your faith should not fail; and when you have returned to Me, strengthen your brethren." – Luke 22:31-32*

There are a few things to point out here. First, Satan is asking to test Simon Peter's faith, as he did Job's. Second, Jesus is indicating it is entirely possible that Peter's faith *could* fail, otherwise, why would He feel the need to pray for Him? Third, Jesus *knew* Peter's faith would fail temporarily, because Jesus told Peter he was going to deny Him three times (verse 34); which Peter did end up doing (verses 54-60). And fourth, the Greek word for 'returned' is epistrepho (ep-ee-stref-o) and it means to revert back, to be converted again.

This is indicating that when Peter denied Jesus publicly three times, it changed the way God considered whether Peter had saving faith in Christ or not. God does not play favorites (Romans 2:11), and His Word says if we publicly deny Jesus, He will deny us before God the Father (Matthew 10:33). Doesn't this truth from God's Word apply to Peter too? Of course it does, which is why Jesus restores Peter, (converts him again) by asking Peter three times if he loves Him (John 21:15-17).

> *"At this point many of His disciples turned away and deserted Him. Then Jesus turned to the twelve and asked, "Are you also going to leave?" – John 6:66-67, NLT*

Jesus had just said some things like His body is real food and His blood is real drink, that the only way to be saved is to have the Holy Spirit, and that human effort is worthless in trying to get to heaven. This was the response, 'many of His disciples turned away and deserted Him.' We don't need to look at the Greek words for 'turned away' and 'deserted.' We know they lost their salvation at that point; but don't miss the fact that God does not force anyone to stay faithful to Him. He asked His twelve disciples if they were going to desert Him too. The decision is always ours to stay with Christ through faith, or to go, and lose our salvation.

My brothers and sisters, by my count I am well over fifty passages from God's Word showing that it is indeed possible for a person to go from being under God's saving grace through faith, to not being under it anymore; either because of a change in that person's faith, or through persistent willful disobedience that is viewed as a lack of faith by God. I have fulfilled my pledge to you. My prayer is that anyone who reads this book will come to an understanding of how important it is for everyone in God's church to want to hear the words, "Well done, good and faithful servant," when they meet Jesus for the first time face to face, in order for the church to function the way it should in this world. And I also pray that you, dear reader, have been encouraged and better equipped now to carry out God's will for you as a part of His church. Amen.

Footnotes / Asterisks

Introduction –
1. U Turn: Restoring America to the Strength of its Roots, George Barna and David Barton, Frontline, Charisma Media / Charisma House Book Group, 2014, page 42
2. Ibid, page 139
3. Ibid, pages 145-146
4. Ibid, pages 145-146
5. Ibid, page 138
6. Ibid, page 144
7. Ibid, page 146
8. Ibid, pages 153-154
9. Ibid, page 149
10. Ibid, pages 147-148
11. Ibid, page 139
12. Ibid, page 139

Chapter 1 –
- Both asterisks – How Much Time Has God Given This World, Charles Kenneth, Advantage Books, chapter 4

Chapter 2 –
- Asterisk – Ibid, chapter 4

Chapter 3 –
- Asterisk – Ibid, chapter 6
- Asterisk # 2 - Ibid, chapter 2

Chapter 5 –
1. U Turn: Restoring America to the Strength of its Roots, George Barna and David Barton, Frontline, Charisma Media / Charisma House Book Group, 2014, page 139
- Asterisk – How Much Time Has God Given This World, Charles Kenneth, Advantage Books, chapter 5

Chapter 7 –
- Asterisks – Ibid, appendix

Chapter 8 –
- Asterisk – Ibid, chapter 6

Chapter 9 –
- Asterisk – Ibid, chapters 4, 6

Chapter 11 –
1. The Karamazov Brothers, Fyodor Dostoevsky, Wordsworth Editions, 2007, page 275
- Asterisk – How Much Time Has God Given This World, Charles Kenneth, Advantage Books, chapter 5

Chapter 12 –
1. More of God, R.T. Kendall, Charisma House, 2019, page 103

Appendix –
- Asterisk – How Much Time Has God Given This World, Charles Kenneth, Advantage Books, 2019, chapter 1

For more information contact Advantage Books via email at info@advbooks.com

To purchase additional copies of this book visit our bookstore website at: www.advbookstore.com

Longwood, Florida, USA
"we bring dreams to life"™
www.advbookstore.com

www.ingramcontent.com/pod-product-compliance
Lightning Source LLC
Chambersburg PA
CBHW070155100426
42743CB00013B/2914